Distant Healing
A COMPLETE GUIDE

Also by Jack Angelo

Your Healing Power: A Comprehensive Guide to Channeling Your Healing Energies

The Spiritual Healing Handbook: How to Develop Your Healing Powers and Increase Your Spiritual Awareness (with Jan Angelo)

Distant Healing
A COMPLETE GUIDE

JACK ANGELO

SOUNDS TRUE
Boulder, Colorado

Sounds True, Inc.
Boulder, CO 80306

SOUNDS TRUE is a trademark of Sounds True, Inc.

All rights reserved. No part of this book may be used or reproduced
in any manner without written permission from the author and publisher.

Copyright © 2008 by Jack Angelo

First published in Great Britain in 2007 by
Piatkus Books Ltd.
5 Windmill Street, London W1T 2JA
e-mail: info@piatkus.co.uk

Cover design by Karen Polaski
Book design by Rachael Tomich

Printed in Canada

10 9 8 7 6 5 4 3 2 1

Library of Congress Cataloging-in-Publication Data
Angelo, Jack.
    Distant healing : a complete guide / Jack Angelo. — 2nd ed.
        p. cm.
    Includes index.
    ISBN 978-1-59179-608-4 (pbk.)
    1. Mental healing. 2. Spiritual healing. I. Title.
        RZ401.A656 2008
        615.8'51--dc22
    Library of Congress Control Number 2008007155

⊕ This book is printed on recycled paper containing 100% post-consumer waste
and processed without chlorine.

Contents

Exercises

Part Four

Illustrations

My thanks to all the workshop participants and all those I have sent healing to over the years—you are a vital part of this book; Jan Angelo, for her support and inspiration; Elspeth Samuel, who rescued me from computer failure; Judy Piatkus, Gill Bailey, and the team at Piatkus Books for their great help in making it possible to give this book to the world; and Rob Hume, editor of *Birds*, for permission to quote from the article mentioned in Chapter 11. I would also like to thank Haven Iverson for her invaluable editing help in the preparation of this U.S. edition.

Love is an energy with the power to unite, harmonize, and heal, and it is unconditional in its action. Distant Healing is the transmission of this energy, through a person's desire and intention to help, to where it is needed. Instead of being present, as in hands-on healing or other forms of energy therapy, the subject is at some distance from the healer—hence "distant healing." (When Distant Healing is capitalized, it refers to the special method and techniques described in this book.)

The great advantage of this form of healing is that the "subject" can be a person, an animal, a plant, an environment, or even a situation. This book explains how Distant Healing works, how to do it, what happens during the process, and the different ways in which it can be used. Distant Healing can be applied to friends and family, pets and the home, the environment, and societal and global problems. The book is accessible, at a number of levels, to anyone interested in healing energies and to all who want to work with those energies. This includes beginners, as well as practicing energy workers, therapists, and health-care professionals.

The Distant Healing Perspective

From the Distant Healing perspective, healing energies come from the Source of all energy—a Oneness, which religious people call God. The energies thus originate *outside* the space-time frame of the physical level and are not governed by its laws until they enter this level. This means they can travel to another person, another being, landscape, or situation, at any distance from us, in an instant.

Why Distant Healing?

There are factors and situations where hands-on help is just not possible. For example, distance prevents certain people from traveling. This is the case with the disabled, those in some kind of confinement, those with a mental or behavioral condition, the sick, and of course those who live just too far away. As a Distant Healer, none of these factors presents a barrier to your being able to offer help.

Similarly, because it is able to work at an energetic level, Distant Healing is an ideal way to address the two urgent issues of our time—environmental and societal problems, whether local or global.

The feeling that you want to help another or do something about a situation is the instinct to heal. When people ask me if they need special qualifications to work as a Distant Healer, I assure them that the most important qualification is this instinct, which comes from the heart.

The Instinct to Heal

I have always been fascinated by the fact that people in all cultures throughout recorded time have been laying hands on others to ease pain, to relieve symptoms, and often to completely heal a condition. This is not surprising when you consider that when we hurt ourselves, our first instinct is to put our hands on it. When this happened to us as children, our mother opened her arms to cuddle us and "kiss it better." This instinct is a loving gesture that comes before any rational thought of what to do about it. You don't need to think about how to be loving or supportive; you just do it.

In the mid-1980s, I was encouraged to discover what this meant in practice. Months of chronic back trouble and sciatica had baffled my doctor, and he suggested that I visit a spiritual healer. "After all," he said, "what have you got to lose?" After two short sessions of hands-on work with the healer, my back trouble was considerably improved, and I pondered how it was done. But my visits had convinced me that I already knew how hands-on healing was done. I had been doing it for others since I was a child.

Discovering Subtle Energies

My encounter with this healer proved to be life changing. I was a curious patient, and Dennis, my healer, did his best to answer my questions but assured me that I would make my own discoveries. This launched me into the world of healing and subtle energy medicine—the therapies that work with "subtle" energies. Subtle energies travel at speeds beyond the speed of light, so they are not visible to normal sight and everyday sensing. Because of this, some people have found this fact of life difficult to understand or accept.

I had been aware of these energies ever since I could remember; sometimes I "saw" them, but more often than not, I sensed them in some other way. For example, I saw light around people. When they were angry or unhappy, this light became frighteningly dark. When I sat with old people, my hands would sometimes tingle or get warm. To me, this type of awareness was quite normal, and I assumed that everyone was like me. As I grew up, I discovered that we all have the natural ability to sense subtle energies, even if we don't exercise it. It is exciting to realize that healing energies fall into this category. They are subtle, but they can certainly be sensed or felt by most of us.

The healer described his work as the action of love. This energy came from the Source, then traveled through him and into the patient. It was love that did the healing. He saw this as complementary to everyday medicine and not as an alternative or last resort for the desperate. Dennis's assertion that love could heal did not sound corny to me—it sounded obvious, but I had never heard any sort of therapy described in this way before.

Healing at a Distance

Quite soon after my time with Dennis, I had the chance to consider his point of view and to put it into practice while on a trip to Italy. Readers of *Your Healing Power* may recall this story. I repeat it here because it tells how I started distant healing and how, in this field of therapy, you can expect the unexpected. I spent my first night in the beautiful Tuscan town of San

Gimignano in a family home. As I lay awake planning the research I was to do in the coming month, little did I know that I was beginning a life in healing. The house had been quiet for some time when suddenly a rasping sound broke the silence. Grandfather Fanciulli was coughing. On and on he coughed, until the coughs changed to groans and cries of desperation. The rest of the house remained still. No one went to his aid. Perhaps the family slept through it because they were already used to these harrowing sounds, and they felt powerless to bring him any form of relief.

I wanted to help him. I was lying on my back, and something made me put my hands outside my bedclothes as if I could send some "healing" toward the grandfather. To my surprise, my palms and fingertips began tingling—a feeling at once strange yet oddly familiar. I mentally asked for help to be sent to the old man. The next moment his coughing stopped abruptly. The house returned to silence, and I dropped off to sleep.

In the small hours of the next night, the old man began to cough again, hardly able to pause for breath, until it sounded as if he would cough up his whole body. There was no space for a groan or a cry. Again I stretched out my hands and asked for help to come to him, and again his coughing stopped immediately.

The same thing happened every night until I left San Gimignano. As I said goodbye to the Fanciullis, old Nonno gave me a smile that seemed to say he knew what had been happening. Perhaps on some level he did know. This first attempt at Distant Healing taught me that whatever was making my hands tingle could be sent somewhere to help. I did not need to analyze how this could happen. During the rest of my time in Italy, I frequently felt the need to send healing thoughts out to people I passed in the street. I guessed that this was healing at a distance, distant healing, and it seemed such an easy way to help out.

Working as a Distant Healer

On my return to my home in Wales, the locality of a small mining village seemed a daunting place when faced with what needed to be done. The land and the people were trying to recover from centuries of mining and now from the trauma of closure and unemployment. A clever, mocking voice in my head seemed to be saying, *Come on, Jack. What can you do here with distant healing?* Something needed to happen to balance my innate skepticism. I joined a local meditation group. The leader said she sensed that I had the gift of healing and suggested I send distant healing to a list of people she had drawn up. She did not tell me how to do this; instead, she said that I would be "inspired from within" to find my own way intuitively.

One evening after a meeting of the meditation group, a young woman came up to me. She was obviously pregnant. She had heard I was a healer and wondered if I could help her. Her boyfriend had left her, her parents had thrown her out of their home, and the fetus kept returning to the breech position, even after being turned by the midwife. Without wondering how, I said I would do my best to help her; I would work out how to assist her later. That night, I sat quietly in a chair. Using my breathing to help me relax, I attuned to the Source. When I felt centered, I asked the Source if I could help the young woman.

With closed eyes, I soon sensed the body of a woman as if it were lying in front of me, hovering in midair. Instead of being surprised, I assumed this was part of the process and relied on my instinct to heal. My palms were already tingling. As I reached out, I could feel her baby in her womb; other unknown hands gently turned the baby so that the head faced downward again. This was accompanied by an overwhelming sense that everything would be all right for mother and baby. I sat for a while, just absorbing the experience. Suddenly the feeling came to hand over their fate to the higher power that seemed to be looking after them. I got up and thought no more about it.

I didn't see the young woman for a while. Then, a few months later, she turned up at the group meeting again. She had a few things to report. Her baby boy had eventually turned into the right position, never returned to breech, and was born naturally. Her boyfriend came to her hospital bedside and asked her to marry him. "What wonderful news!" I said. But that wasn't all. Her parents seemed to have had a change of heart too, because they also visited her and welcomed her back to their home. I heard the list in amazement. So this was the world of Distant Healing!

Sometimes I sent help and nothing seemed to happen. I had to learn not to take it personally when people didn't bother to report back one way or the other. But during the ensuing weeks, positive feedback from many of those who had requested my help gave me proof that Distant Healing was effective for all kinds of concerns.

Becoming Aware of the Energies

When I sat to do distant healing, I was aware of an energetic change in my hands, which signaled to me that I was working. But this was not always accompanied by a sense of the presence of the person who needed the help. When I did sense the person, I was able to sense the body from whatever angle seemed necessary. I knew where I needed to place my hands on the body, and the organs concerned gave off information about what was wrong. I often saw or felt what was taking place as the healing progressed. In this way, I was able to work with people as if they were physically present. I also picked up a range of messages coming from different parts of a person's body. These told not only of the physical conditions but also of worries, sadness, stress, past traumas, life incidents, unfulfilled needs, as if everything that had happened to that person was recorded somewhere in the body or in the energy field of that body.

Part One of this book will prepare you for experiences like these. In Part Two, we will look at these experiences in detail to see how they can contribute to more advanced work.

My Healing Journey

My journey as a healing practitioner began with distant healing. I kept a working journal and built a very useful database of experiences that gave me an excellent grounding and understanding when I began to work "hands on." My interest in the natural world led me to work with the healing ways of many indigenous peoples, especially Native Americans. Even though I was able to work with these "medicine" people for only a few days at a time, I found that they were able to transmit further teachings at a distance. Sometimes I would wake up and grab paper and pencil, realizing I had just received a teaching during my sleep. This book also includes some of the knowledge gained from my indigenous, or "shamanic," encounters.

During twenty-five years of "hands-on" subtle energy work, I have written a number of books on the subject, including *Your Healing Power*, which has become an international healing classic. Its sequel, *The Spiritual Healing Handbook*, appeals to those who want to take the work even further. Things have now come full circle and distant healing is again my main therapeutic focus.

The Next Step for Healers—Distant Healing

The dozen or so years since *Your Healing Power* was published in 1994 have given those who have used my books time to achieve a good level of proficiency in healing. This has prepared them for the next important step in healing—to work with situations where hands-on healing is difficult or impossible. The field of energy medicine has been considerably expanded now that two further, but crucial, issues present themselves. Their call to us is urgent, and there is little time for us to stop and think about what to do—our response must be immediate, just as it must be when a child has fallen and lies crying. These issues concern our global environment, the Earth, and the fear that fuels chaos and violence everywhere on this beautiful planet. This is why this book is needed now.

How to Use the Book

Start your practice, like I did, by learning how to send healing to another person or a favorite pet. With exercises at each stage, the book will guide you carefully, giving you a firm foundation from which you can move to the more advanced work in Part Two. Stay with each section until you feel confident with the practice.

You will have many experiences once you start work, and Chapters 7, 8, and 9 are designed to prepare you for them. You can start your Distant Healing work straight away and dip into these later chapters when you feel the need. Keeping a journal of your progress will allow you to maintain your own record of what you do and the results that you observe. This will help you build your own database of experience.

About the Exercises

The exercises are designed to lead you to the point where you will feel confident making Distant Healing a life skill. The exercises with a partner are essential for developing your knowledge base but are not essential to your work as a caring individual. Your knowledge base can be acquired over time by practicing when the opportunity arises.

You may find it helpful to tape or digitally record some of the exercises so that you can carry them out without referring back to the book. Or your working partner can read them out for you.

Interaction with a partner or a group as you practice Distant Healing adds the extra dimension of being with others, which is so helpful in developing an open and compassionate heart. But there may be reasons why you have to work on your own. When this is the case, it is worth recalling that you care about others because you are aware of them and their needs, and you are aware of being part of a diverse global family. Through Distant Healing, you essentially interact with others so that you are an effective and vital contributor to individual and world healing. Meanwhile, it is important not to let your lack of a working partner stop you from making a start with Distant Healing. You will soon see that the exercises for individual practice will prepare you to work quite adequately.

Practice the exercises and experiment with the techniques in the book to find out how Distant Healing works. Sooner or later a pattern will emerge that will indicate that you are creating your own individual practice.

Please note that none of the exercises should be used for purposes other than those specified.

part one

Chapter 1

Widening Our Circle of Compassion

What Is Distant Healing?

For millennia, healing at a distance has been a time-honored way of ministering to the sick and needy. Evidence from around the world shows that this form of healing has always been just as common as hands-on healing. Among the Middle Eastern peoples of the first century CE, for example, two famous healers from Galilee are recorded as working this way: the healing of the great Gamli'el's son by Hanina ben Dosa (in Babylonian Talmud: Berakhot 34b) and the healing of the royal official's son by Yeshua/ Jesus (in John 4:46–53).

People with different worldviews or religious beliefs have different ways of defining distant healing and of explaining how it works and the energies with which they work. Moreover, each worldview has a different language to describe the process. At an individual level, people's life experience and their at-oneness with their own life journey influence these views and definitions. However, all worldviews incorporate our instinct to offer help to one another. We can do this by thought, by what we say, and by what we do.

Your instinct to heal means that you may often send out a thought or prayer that healing will be directed to a person, an animal, the environment, or a situation. In Distant Healing, we further strengthen this simple, but loving, impulse with the power of spiritual intention. Here, the Distant Healer is able to both channel and transmit healing energies through conscious attunement to the Source of these energies.

How Distant Healing Works—The Healing Triangle

In the first stage of Distant Healing, we attune to, or align ourselves with, the source of all energy—Oneness. This can happen in a variety of ways— from being in nature, to losing ourselves in a creative task, to the simple method in the first exercise, on page 17. You will know when this has happened; you will sense it as a feeling of being centered and serene, relaxed yet alert. Once you are attuned, you are in a state of readiness to create the links that allow healing energy to flow.

When you form, for example, the healing intention that you would like to send to a loved one, you make an energetic link with that person. This, in turn, opens up the link between your loved one (the subject) and the Source. You have effectively set up what I call the Healing Triangle.

Connecting to the Source bridges the spiritual level, from where healing energies originate, and the physical level of the space-time frame, where they are needed. The subject in the Healing Triangle is the person, animal, place, or situation you wish to work with. When you link with the subject, you activate the link between the subject and the Source. In the illustration, the Triangle is set within a circle to signify the oneness of all three points and the dedicated protective circle you will be working with. By creating the Healing Triangle, you overcome distance, for love energy has the power to travel both outside and inside the boundaries of space and time.

The healing process begins at the spiritual level. From there it travels "downward" to the other levels of being. This means that sometimes energy will reach the physical instantly and bring about change, but other times energy will be needed on a subtle level first (such as the mental level), and change will be seen more slowly on the physical level. These things depend on the cause (or causes) of the condition, the soul's journey, and the state of readiness of a person, and may involve the balancing factors of the law of cause and effect. When souls decide to address imbalances created in the present life or in past lives, the factors of this law will influence the energetic situation.

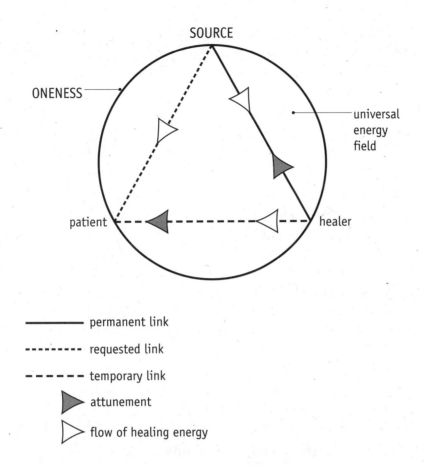

figure 1 **The Healing Triangle**

The Power of Intention

Many researchers, including Dr. Larry Dossey, have shown that intention has a bearing on the outcome of the energetic process (see Further Reading, page 213, and Web Resources, page 217). For this reason, the healing request must be made unconditionally, so that healing is directed to where it is needed and not necessarily how we, with our limited knowledge, think it should be applied. In other words, we simply ask for healing to be sent, without limiting our request to a specific condition. For example, it is more appropriate to ask, "May healing be sent to (name)," rather than "Please cure her cancer."

Remaining unconditional with your request acknowledges the fact that a person is a spiritual being and that it is the spirit that dictates the activities of the healing force. It also honors the soul's evolutionary journey and the deeper reason for a condition about which we actually know nothing. This attitude does not see health as an isolated condition of the body. Instead, we cooperate with the body consciousness, rather than manipulate it.

Distant Healing, Loss, and Illness

As with situations where hands-on healing is either not possible or inappropriate, Distant Healing always helps a person to pass over, to let go of the body. When responding to a request for help over a passing or terminal illness, the Distant Healer is joining the person on this part of his or her journey. In the case of sudden death through accident or injury, this help is invaluable. Healing can also be sent to the bereaved and anyone else affected by the death. There is always a team of people involved in a passing, and they will all benefit from the healing you send to them.

People may also request help over an illness or operation. Here again, the Distant Healer is joining the person on this part of his or her journey. Those supporting ill or disabled people will also benefit from your healing help. And just as in the bereavement situation, there is always a team involved in an illness or operation. Distant Healing will ensure that the team will receive the energetic boost it needs to do its best for the patient.

The Challenge of the Global Community

We are part of a global community, and our relationship with all life on planet Earth becomes evident when news of every distressing event around the world finds its way into our home. Many feel powerless in the face of this information onslaught. While enriching our lives with useful knowledge, the media has at the same time become a source of fear, telling us that life is not safe anymore. We feel that we could do without the constant reminders about crime, societal breakdown, and environmental disaster.

We have to find ways to cope with these stresses. The most common response is to "switch off," to become apathetic or even cynical. Switching off can involve finding something to make us feel good for a while. There are plenty of distractions, and it's easy to become addicted to some of them. Or if we are pessimistic, we won't be constantly disappointed. Unfortunately, coping strategies like these only encourage us to live in fear.

In the last century, the celebrated physicist and Nobel Prize winner Albert Einstein, forced by persecution to flee from Germany to Britain and then America, understood such feelings. A letter he wrote in 1950 shows that he recognized that most of us, though part of a spiritual whole, nevertheless experience a deep sense of separation from everything and everyone else. But, Einstein insisted, we can break free from these feelings by widening "our circle of compassion to embrace all living creatures and the whole of nature in its beauty." This phrase resonates with me as a description of Distant Healing, because it embraces the traditional role of reaching out to the sick and needy, as well as the new agenda of Distant Healing, which widens "our circle of compassion" to address the urgent problems of our time. This form of compassionate action is a spiritual activity that strengthens and maintains our spiritual core.

Distant Healing—An Essential Life Skill

Our reconnection with the sacred gives progressively more meaning to life and our part in it and provides the foundations for a sustainable civilization. As Distant Healing enlarges the traditional role of healing, it emerges as an essential life skill for all those who wish to bring harmony and well-being to the twenty-first century.

For practicing healers and therapists already making a contribution, this book will provide a wider context and will enhance your practice. However, you don't have to be a trained therapist to participate—you just have to want to do it.

A Way into Healing

Distant Healing could be your way back to empowerment and a way into helping or healing; it may become an important addition to your therapeutic repertoire, or it may become the healing practice that you prefer. It will always be a source of self-discovery as well as of revealing how healing works. Distant Healing allows you to work quietly and anonymously, or it can introduce you to a world, people, and situations you would never have met otherwise—it's your choice.

You will find that you do not need to go looking for people or places to heal. The law of attraction means that people will seek your help, because the time is right for both of you to meet, as your individual paths cross. The meeting has a sacred dimension because it has been arranged at a soul level with the agreement of all concerned. In this way, Distant Healing can help heal the world as well as people, heal the landscape as well as animals and plants, heal situations as well as conditions. Your heart will direct you and show you how to heal the place that hurts, whatever form that place may take.

Trusting Your Experience

My Distant Healing experiences are part of my own spiritual journey. Your experiences will be unique to you and should be treated as such. There are few rules and norms in subtle energy work apart from attuning to the Source of healing, realizing that all with whom you will work are a manifestation of that Oneness, and working from the heart. In this way, your inner self will guide you to the methods that are best for you. If you observe what happens and keep a careful record, that record will become your own database. You will learn what you need to learn and do what you need to do. It is important to keep an open mind, because your inner promptings may be to work with other beings and situations that you might not have otherwise considered.

Sooner or later you will be faced with the question, Is it right to send help to those who have not requested it? You will have to make your own decision. I have found that a good strategy, whenever any decision has to be made, is to ask your heart, What would love do? My own answer is that love would want to help in some way. I also know that because healing energies first engage with the soul concerned, that soul can decide whether or not to accept help. If your help is rejected, it will simply be passed on to a place where it can do some good. Nothing is lost.

In my practice over the years, I have met very few of the people with whom I have worked. Many live on the other side of the world. Most often I receive a request for help from someone close to the person concerned. In those cases, I always ask for feedback to be given on a regular basis so that I know how the person is progressing. Even so, you can be sure that people forget to do this, and you will be left wondering how they are. This is why I find it most helpful to do my best and then leave it in the capable hands of the spiritual powers concerned, without giving the work any further thought.

Attunement

Because Distant Healing is about taking action, let's pause at this point to take stock and try the first exercise, which is about the experience of attunement, or alignment, with the Source. This exercise can be carried out indoors or outdoors.

---

exercise 1 ATTUNEMENT

Attunement for Distant Healing is aligning your individual self with the Higher Self, or soul, and with the energies of healing. This consists of effective posture, effective breathing, relaxed awareness, and focus. You will need to bring your focus to your *heart center*, or the subtle energy center in the middle of your chest. We will study this energy center in detail later. For now, think of it as the place where your soul, or Higher Self, takes up residence.

First, notice how you are sitting and how you are breathing. Are you aware of anything going on around you? These awarenesses will soon become second nature once you begin practicing the exercises.

The way we breathe and the way we use our breath are the keys to how we energize ourselves. They even affect the way we think. Our breathing, in turn, is influenced by our posture. From here on we'll choose the best posture for relaxed, but effective, breathing. This will ensure effective energy circulation.

In all the exercises, "relaxed" never means slumped or stooped. Relaxed means without tension, hanging loose, while remaining alert in your attention to the world.

• Sit far back in your chair, or cross-legged on the ground, so that the two girdles of the pelvis and shoulders are in line. Your spine should

exercise continues >

---

be straight, without pushing the chest forward. Hold your head up without straining. Rest your hands, palms up, on your thighs. If sitting in a chair, keep your feet flat on the floor, feeling your connection with the ground. This is your connection with the Earth.

- Close your eyes, while remaining totally alert. Using your breath, relax your body. With each out-breath relax your pelvis, feeling yourself sinking into the chair. Relax your shoulders and the back of your neck.

- Breathe naturally through your nose. Keep your mouth lightly closed with the jaws unclenched. Put the front of your tongue against the hard palate, just behind your top front teeth, and then let it settle into its own position.

- Breathe gently into your abdomen and enjoy the feeling of being relaxed yet alert. Whenever you take up the sitting posture, this is the state you will need to achieve.

- Bring your focus to your heart center. Now, relaxed, but fully aware, and breathing naturally, allow yourself to be at one with your Higher Self. Spend a few moments in union with Oneness, recalling that your Higher Self (or soul) is at one with the Source.

- Allow all thoughts to pass through your mind unobstructed. Any sounds around you are simply the accompaniment to your attunement. You are in the world. Nothing disturbs you. You are at one with the Source (or whatever is your concept of the Source).

- Give thanks to the Source for the opportunity to be used as a channel for healing. Ask to be as pure a channel as possible. Ask for

exercise continues >

protection for yourself and all the people, beings, and situations you will be engaging with. Dedicate yourself and your work and ask for it to be blessed. Add any other prayers you wish, aware that you and the Source are one.

Aids to Attunement

Your attunement, with your focus in the heart center, will be the key element in all your Distant Healing work. Because attunement means aligning yourself with the sacred, use whatever helps you arrive at that state. Dedicating and preparing your work space will begin the process, but you may find that things like lighting incense, listening to music, sitting in front of your shrine, chanting, praying, or using musical instruments or a short meditation can all be means to achieving alignment. I find that when I am outdoors, the mere presence of the natural world helps me attune very quickly. Experiment to find out what works for you.

Through conscious attunement, you make your link with your Higher Self and the Source of healing energies. As I described earlier, this activates the first side of a very powerful energetic structure—the Healing Triangle. When you link with the subject to whom you are going to send Distant Healing, you activate the second side. This, in turn, opens up the subject's own link with the Source to activate the third side of the Healing Triangle.

When I began Distant Healing, I knew I was in an attuned state of readiness because of what my hands were telling me. We may be at a distance from our subject, but our hands still have an important role to play in the work. This is because they have a direct energetic link with our heart center. In the next chapter, we'll build on the experience of attunement to discover the role of the hands in Distant Healing.

Chapter 2

Your Healing Hands

In this chapter, you will become acquainted with your *healing hands.* This begins a relationship with your hands that will continue to develop as you work your way through the book.

Our hands always let us know how we feel in our heart. If we love someone, the chances are that we will want to touch them. Pet owners reinforce the bond with their furry friends by stroking them. Yet the urge to use our hands to hurt someone or something is a sure indicator that we have lost contact with love and affection.

Healing reveals the energetic link between the hands and the heart, and although Distant Healing begins with thought and intention, our hands become a useful guide when we work this way. Our hands lead us where healing energy is needed because they have a subtle sensing apparatus that is sensitive to energy flow and imbalance. If we cooperate with it, this sensing mechanism will be activated and guided by the power of intuition—a faculty of our Higher Self. If you practice allowing the sensitivity of your hands to work in tandem with your intuition, your hands will prove to be a guide and helper you can trust.

It is possible to activate the subtle sensing centers of your palms. Your palms have a direct link with the heart energy center, and activation helps prepare the hands for any subtle or therapeutic work, including Distant Healing. So we begin our new relationship with the hands with a few exercises.

---

exercise 2 ACTIVATING THE PALM CENTERS

- First, take a good look at your hands. Turn them over slowly so that you see both the surfaces of the back of the hands and of the palms. Try to look at them as if you are seeing them for the first time. These are your tools for reaching out and helping others.

- Now close both hands to make loose fists, squeezing the tips of the fingers against the palms. Squeeze and let go. Do this a number of times in rapid succession until both hands feel energized. The same result may be achieved by gently rubbing your palms together in a circular motion. You may feel a tingling or warmth in your palms. Remember this sensation.

With this next simple activation exercise, you are ready to get to know how your hands react to subtle energies.

---

exercise 3 SENSING THE QUALITY OF YOUR HANDS' ENERGIES

- Stand or sit comfortably. Take three full breaths into your abdomen to energize yourself.

- Hold your hands up at about waist height, with your palms facing toward each other and the width of your body between them. Let your hands relax so that the fingers separate naturally. Notice what you sense between your two palms.

exercise continues >

- Bring your hands together slowly, again noticing what you sense as you do so.

- Try again with your hands stretched a little wider apart. This time imagine that the energies are like strands of elastic stretching from hand to hand.

- Vary the distance between your hands. Turn them over. Move your hands together in different ways. Note the various sensations.

figure 2 **Sensing Your Hands' Energies**

If you can find an interested partner, get them to help you work with another pair of hands, as in the next exercise.

exercise 4 **SENSING THE ENERGIES OF A PARTNER'S HANDS**

- Stand opposite your partner at a distance such that you can just touch each other's palms when your arms are fully extended. You and your partner should hold your palms up at about chest height,

exercise continues >

with elbows bent, so that your palms face your partner's palms. Let your hands relax so that your fingers separate naturally.

- Slowly move your right palm to meet your partner's left palm. Then move your left palm to meet your partner's right palm. Gently pull your palms back toward you. Let your partner try these same movements. These are the same kind of movements you tried in the previous exercise.

- Now both of you move both sets of palms together. Slowly pull them back again. Notice what you sense. Was it different from sensing your own energies? Discuss the sensations with your partner.

Your hands are receptive to energies, as you have experienced. Let's see what happens when you encourage this process with visualization.

exercise 5 **BREATHING ENERGY INTO THE HANDS**

- Sit comfortably with your feet flat on the ground. Rest your hands on your thighs, palms up. (There is an energy center in your palm that is receptive to subtle energies. By keeping your palms up, you are in receptive mode). Breathe normally. Relax your elbows, the back of your neck, and your shoulders. Do this by letting go with each out-breath. Close your eyes if this helps you concentrate.

- Focus on the center of your palms. Visualize energy as light beaming down into them. Note what you feel or sense.

- Now visualize that you can breathe this energy into your palms.

exercise continues >

As you see the energy beaming down, breathe in. On the in-breath, the energy is absorbed into your hands. On the out-breath, it fills your hands and arms.

figure 3 **Breathing Energy into the Hands**

Note your sensations and compare them with the first part of the exercise. Follow this with the next exercise.

exercise 6 **SENDING OUT ENERGY FROM YOUR HANDS**

- Sitting in the same position as in the previous exercise, raise your

exercise continues >

hands to about chest height with your palms facing away from the body.

- Visualize that you can beam energy *out* from your palms. What do you sense?

- Fill your hands with energy on the in-breath as you did in the previous exercise. Send out the energy on the out-breath.

figure 4 **Sending Out Energy from the Hands**

exercise 7 **SENDING ENERGY TO A PARTNER**

- Sit opposite your partner, who should be sitting at least six feet away from you. Both of you hold your hands up to about chest height, with the elbows bent and the palms facing toward each other. Ask your partner to remain receptive. Take three full breaths into your abdomen to energize yourself.

- Breathe in. On the out-breath, send energy from your hands to the palms of your partner's hands. Repeat.

- Now try beaming energy to your partner's hands by thought alone. Note all your sensations.

Change roles, with your partner carrying out each stage of the exercise. Again, note your sensations. What did receiving energy from your partner feel like? Compare notes together.

Experiencing Subtle Energies—The Early Stages

You are beginning to experience what happens to your hands when they are in contact with subtle energy; for example, you might feel a tingling sensation or heat. Others report experiencing a slight trembling or seeing colored lights. This is what might happen when you are ready to work. One of the signals that your work is complete may be the cessation of tingling or heat. Make a note of the signals that your hands give—they will be personal to you, and they may be your own signal that you are ready to begin.

These sensations show that you have begun to experience subtle energies and some of the subtle aspects of your own, and perhaps your partner's, body. The following chapter provides you with the next essential step in understanding and appreciating your "light" body.

Chapter 3

Your Light Body

Your healing work will bring you into contact with many aspects of human life—and perhaps other life forms as well. It is quite natural to find yourself pondering, Who am I? Where did I come from? What really is a body?

Let's look more closely, then, at the person we think we are.

The Body Is a Spiritual Creation

The Distant Healer acknowledges that Earth exists as a unique destination for the journeying soul and as such needs to be honored and celebrated. Each of us, when we come to Earth, embarks on a life adventure that will be unique to us. We do not know where anyone else is on their soul journey. We do not know why people or situations present themselves as they do. What we do know is that when we send out Distant Healing, we are journeying together for a time. For these reasons, our work is always unconditional.

Soul, or our Higher Self, first has contact with creation through an energy pattern that can be envisaged as a "body" of light. This light is vibrating at a frequency far beyond the speed of physical light and is another term for "spirit," or the energy of the Source. But to engage in the total experience of physicality, a soul needs the much denser energy form of the physical body.

To be conscious of our physical state, we also have the mental abilities of mind—the capability to create thought; intelligence, which determines the level and quality of thought; and will, the power to drive thought into action. Mental energies travel at a far greater speed than light, and they vibrate at a far greater frequency than the body; thus, mental energies can project beyond the body, creating an energy body invisible to normal sight but detectable by our subtle senses. All thoughts—their actions, interactions, and reactions—are processed in this mental body.

When positive or negative thoughts interact with physical life, emotions are generated by the individual personality. These emotional energies, though not vibrating as fast as thought, still vibrate at a far greater rate than the physical body and so, again, project beyond it, creating another energy body. In this energy body, our emotions and emotional reactions are processed. Feelings generated by the Higher Self, to act as signals of warning, confirmation, or guidance, are also processed in this emotional part of our being.

Thus our spiritual, mental, and emotional levels, or bodies, all vibrate at speeds greater than the speed of light. Their energies are *subtle*. As you have already found, they can be detected through the subtle senses. This is also true of other beings, such as animals—you may have noticed this with a pet. We all have this natural ability, which is actually essential to our survival. If you were not already aware of it, you will find that practicing Distant Healing is a good way to reactivate this ability.

There are vast differences between the vibratory frequencies of the body and the frequencies of our spiritual, mental, and emotional levels. The *etheric* level acts as a bridge between the body and these subtle levels.

For Distant Healers, the physical body, with its symptoms, is usually the presenting problem. But you may also be asked to help people with emotional, mental, or even spiritual issues, all of which originate at one of the subtle levels described in one or more of the subtle bodies.

The Human Energy Field

I have described human beings as spiritual beings with an energy pattern designed for manifesting and experiencing life at the physical level—here on planet Earth and in the rest of the universe. Because of its various energies, this energy pattern appears as a *series* of energy bodies. This may give the impression that, energetically, we are something like a set of Russian dolls, of bodies within bodies. The important distinction between the different energetic levels is that the different rates of vibration allow the various bodies to be interpenetrating rather than simply sitting one inside the other.

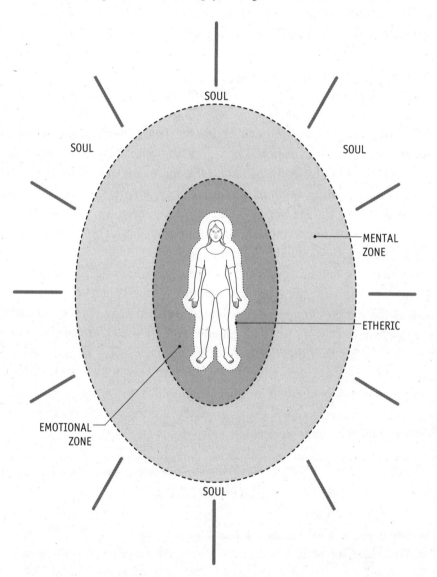

figure 5 **The Human Energy Field**

In other words, the soul part of you is right where you are. So are the mental, emotional, and etheric parts of you. In reality, all these aspects are one, aspects of the whole you. Each body radiates its specific energies, creating a total field around you, known to the ancient Greeks as the *aura*. This aura appears as a glowing emanation that some people sense as different moving colors; others may sense the field as sound, feelings, indescribable sensations, or personal information, such as a recent experience.

Encountering Another Energy Field

When we encounter another person, we tend to decide very quickly if we like him or her or whether that person will be good for us. At a subtle level, we immediately sense the person's energy field, which gives us instant information about him or her. How your energies relate to those of another person is the basis of compatibility. Of course our mind can, and often does, override our intuition or subtle sensing. Perhaps the subtle information is negative, yet the person actually *looks* nice to us. We can choose whether to listen to the message from our intuition or the one from our mind. These factors apply to situations, too.

All situations have an energy field. We can be aware of the information in the field, or not, and take appropriate action, or not. When we are asked for help as Distant Healers, we are presented with a person within a situation. Because we try to work unconditionally, we may wish to accept each case as it comes. But this does not prevent us from acting on an inner prompting not to accept a certain case. There may be a reason for not choosing to work with a person or situation that will unfold later.

Let's make some practical discoveries about energy fields. You will need a partner for the next exercise.

exercise 8 **SENSING THE ENERGY FIELD**

- See if you can locate the edge or boundary of your partner's field. Your partner should stand in a relaxed position and breathe

exercise continues >

normally without focusing on what you are doing. Stand a good ten paces away from your partner. Relax by letting go of any tensions on the out-breath. Take as long as you need.

- Hold your hands up in front of you, with your arms bent and your palms facing your partner. Put your attention into your activated palms (see Exercise 2: Activating the Palm Centers, page 22).

- Now walk very slowly toward your partner. Stop as soon as you feel a slight energetic resistance, as if making contact with the surface of an invisible balloon. You are sensing the edge of your partner's energy field. Move your hands over and around the

figure 6 **Sensing the Energy Field**

exercise continues >

invisible surface so that you get a picture of its shape. Note the shape that you have actually defined (see Figure 6).

- Step back from your partner and relax.

- Hold up your hands again, facing your partner. Now see if you can sense another layer of energy in your partner's field as you move very slowly toward him or her. The more relaxed you are, the easier it will be to sense the denser layers of the field as you move closer to your partner's body.

- Decide how many zones of energy you were able to sense in your partner's field, where they seemed to be located, and what shape they seemed to have.

- Change roles to let your partner work with you. Compare experiences.

The next exercise introduces you to the information stored as various energies in the energy field. Again, you will need to work with a partner. The exercise should last from two to five minutes.

exercise 9 **SENSING INFORMATION IN THE ENERGY FIELD**

- Sit opposite each other without being close enough to touch. Both of you relax and breathe normally. Your partner should be as passive as possible. Both of you close your eyes to avoid absorbing visual information.

exercise continues >

- As you sit opposite your partner, realize that his or her energy field includes mental and emotional material. Allow yourself to be open to this material and see if you become aware of it.

- Visualize that your whole body is open to this energetic material. What are you aware of? Make a mental note of it, no matter how strange or ordinary it may seem.

- Relax for a few minutes and change roles.

- Share and compare notes together.

Exercise 9 may require practice before you are able to sense material in a partner's field. Although you need to be relaxed, you also need to be totally aware. When we come to certain forms of Distant Healing later in the book, you will find that this exercise is particularly useful in preparing you for them.

The Etheric Body

Healing energies make contact with a person at the etheric bridging level. In practice, the etheric body can be seen as a misty layer of light, projecting one to two inches or so beyond the physical body, which is most often visible to normal vision when a person is standing against a white or pale background. The etheric body extends beyond the physical body because its energies are vibrating at a slightly faster rate. The etheric body has a shape somewhat like the human form, with an outer surface composed of a glowing weblike structure, the whole appearing to be illuminated from within.

The luminous depths of the etheric body contain hundreds of even brighter lines of light. These transparent channels permit the flow of a range of subtle energies, which appear as moving streams or threads of light. Where the channels intersect, a node or vortex of light is formed. This gives the etheric body the appearance of a starry sky at night. Many of these etheric channels correspond to the meridians used in acupuncture.

figure 7 **The Etheric Body and the Seven Main Energy Centers**

The nodes of light are the subtle energy centers of the etheric body (see also *chakra* in the Glossary, page 209). The more channels that converge, the larger the energy center and the more prominent its activities. All centers are engaged in some aspect of processing and monitoring of energy flow. The seven main centers are seen to be connected to a central channel aligned with the spine (see Figure 7). Their function is to allow the flow of energy to and from the various levels of our being and to process the energies generated by specific life issues. Because their roles are crucial to human life, and therefore to Distant Healing, we will study them in more detail in Part Two.

Armed with the essential knowledge about your body and its subtle, or light, aspects, you almost have what you need to start with Distant Healing. Before you do that, however, I want to make sure that you begin with the best possible grounding and that you are properly equipped for your healing journey from the outset. These preparations, which you will need from now on, are fundamental.

Chapter 4

Preparations for Getting Started

Taking Up the Challenge

When we make the choice to act (instead of doing nothing) and to send positive energies out to someone or some situation (instead of a negative thought), we take up the challenge of remembering Oneness and the essential nature of our being: Love.

Our action has to be as natural, spontaneous, and unconditional as any other loving or compassionate gesture. This is a step on the way to self-empowerment, yes, but if you find yourself acting in this manner, you can be sure that you have the Distant Healing attitude. It is an attitude that ensures that you will have the motivation and the energy to enjoy practicing Distant Healing.

The work is a two-way process involving many responsibilities—to oneself as well as to the person we are working with. Even though the person may never know we are sending out to him or her, we need to bear in mind that we have entered into the sacred relationship of Distant Healing where both parties are equal. The reality of the other person becomes our reality, and the energetic flow will affect us too.

As I indicated earlier, healing energies work simultaneously at the spiritual, mental, and emotional levels, as well as with the physical body. The energies will tend to go where there is the greatest need, so effects may not necessarily show up on the physical level. This may mean that some of the people we are working with find themselves needing to reassess their lives by looking at what is most important and what their priorities should be; determining what causes distress and what can be done about those causes; and understanding the effects of thoughts and emotions and how much the people are in control of those thoughts and emotions. However, this only occurs because of synchronicity and at the time a person is ready and able to deal with it. We can be assured, too, that the healing process is gentle and loving.

Beginning the Process of Attunement

We can now expand our initial choice to take positive and caring action by applying some conscious preparation. Much of the energy we radiate has been generated by thought and is of a relatively heavy nature. Some of this energy is in the universal energy field around us, some we absorb from other people, and some is transmitted to us via thought. Knowing that we are surrounded by, and absorb, the energies of life—the buildings and objects, situations and people we encounter—we first prepare ourselves to work as Distant Healers by clearing, balancing, and energizing our own energy field. This is the total field of energy that each of us generates from the different levels of our being. This field changes as our life experience changes, moment by moment. Because the Distant Healing process takes place within the energy field, we will look at this field again in Part Two.

Clearing, balancing, and energizing our own energy field begins the process of attunement to the Source of healing energies. As you found in Exercise 1 (page 17), attunement involves aligning your individual self with the Higher Self and the subtle energies. Your level of attunement will determine the quality and quantity of the energy you initiate and channel. The exercises in this chapter will raise your level of attunement and deepen your experience of Exercise 1. Your approach to each exercise should be enthusiastic but totally relaxed. There are no deadlines, and healing is never about competition.

The Benefits of Effective Posture

I mentioned how breathing is the key to energizing ourselves and how breathing is influenced by our posture. The effective standing posture has the same energizing aim—a relaxed body and a relaxed mind, where you can pay attention while letting all thoughts pass through your mind unobstructed. You will practice this stance in the next exercise and will learn to remove any energy that might impede your attunement. The exercise uses the clearing energy of silver light. The "standing stance" opens your energy field and allows energy to flow freely.

exercise 10 **CLEARING THE ENERGY FIELD**

- Stand, or sit if necessary, with your feet shoulder-width apart and your arms hanging loosely by your sides. Gently flex the knees and allow your body to relax. Use your breath to aid with relaxation and attunement.

- As you become aware that your center of gravity is just below the navel, breathe in the same way as in earlier exercises, gently into the abdomen. Enjoy the feeling of being relaxed yet alert. This is the state to aim for whenever an exercise calls for a standing posture.

- Take a moment to be aware of any heavy energy in your body and energy field, noting where it seems to have accumulated. (It is worth making a note of this observation in your journal every time you do this exercise to see if there is a pattern.)

- Now visualize yourself under a shower or gentle waterfall of silver light. Let this light pour over you, through you, and out into your surrounding field, especially to any place where you sensed an accumulation of heavy energy. Allow the light to exit through your hands and feet and every body orifice.

- Notice the color of the light that moves in to fill the space that you

exercise continues >

have cleared. Your awareness of this color will confirm that a clearing is taking place. You might sense this in a number of ways. If you feel you are sensing nothing (it is your mind saying you can't), carry out this important exercise as if you can sense something.

• Note the sensations of clearing and the sensations of being cleansed.

figure 8 **Clearing the Energy Field**

• Continue to breathe naturally and take a few moments to be with these sensations.

Now you are ready to bring balance and stability to your energy field with the next exercise.

exercise 11 **THE RAINBOW BREATH**

Note: Anyone experiencing breathing difficulties should attempt the exercises involving conscious breathing only under supervision.

Before practicing this exercise, refresh your picture of the seven main energy centers (chakras). When in a state of balance, each vibrates to one of the rainbow colors (see Figure 7).

• Stand, or sit if necessary, with your feet shoulder-width apart and your arms hanging loosely by your sides. Relax your body.

• Take three or more breaths to clear the lungs. Allow any tension, worry, or anxiety to exit as you exhale through your open mouth. Close your mouth and breathe normally when you feel settled.

• You are now going to fill your energy field with seven spheres of colored light, ranging from red to violet. Each sphere should be visualized as outside the one you created before.

• Breathe in, visualizing red light rising from behind your heels, moving up your back to the top of your head. Pause for a moment.

• As you exhale, visualize the red light spreading down the front of your body until it is under your feet. You are now enclosed in a sphere of red light and ready to build your personal energy rainbow.

• Breathe up a sphere of orange light, spreading it in the same way by using the breath, making sure it totally encloses the sphere of red light.

exercise continues >

- Breathe up golden yellow light and surround the orange light sphere.

- Breathe up green light and surround the golden yellow light sphere.

- Breathe up sky-blue light and surround the green light sphere.

- Breathe up royal-blue/indigo light and surround the sky-blue light sphere.

- Breathe up violet/purple light and surround the royal blue/indigo light sphere.

- Spend a few moments in silent awareness as you remain totally enclosed in the seven spheres of rainbow light. They are, of course, aspects of the one white light, but by working with them separately, you are able to balance the seven main energy centers of your subtle energy body.

figure 9 **The Rainbow Breath**

exercise continues >

Pausing to be with the effects of this exercise can put you in touch with deep parts of yourself. What do you experience? A sense of peace, of balance, of healing? This is you.

The Breath and Breathing

This brings us to the role of breathing in your life and in your work as a Distant Healer. Although all of us begin breathing from the moment of birth and we know that our life depends on it, most people do not know how to breathe properly; neither do they know about the spiritual dimension of their own breath.

This second aspect of the sacred breath will gradually become apparent as you practice the exercises, most of which use the breath to ease tension; bring balance, calm, and relaxation; and facilitate the attunement process. Correct breathing opens the way for the beneficial presence and influence of the Higher Self. Part of the life skill of Distant Healing is the gift of conscious breathing.

How Breathing Works

The action of the large muscle forming the floor of the chest, the diaphragm, is what allows us to breathe. When the diaphragm is flattened downward, the cavity enclosed by the rib cage is enlarged, creating a vacuum. The lungs are suspended in this cavity, and they immediately expand to fill the space, drawing in air via the nose or mouth. Once the lungs are full, a nervous impulse signals the diaphragm to relax upward. This deflates the lungs, forcing the breath to be expelled.

As air is breathed into the lungs, oxygen passes through fine membranes of the lung into the bloodstream to oxygenate the cells and tissues of the whole body. Waste gases from the bodily processes, such as carbon dioxide, leave the bloodstream via the lungs to be expelled.

There are thus two breaths, the in-breath and the out-breath, each of which has a different sensation and a specific purpose. It is interesting to note that the first thing we do at birth is take an in-breath—we engage with the receptive, or "feminine," energy stream. This is reversed at the death of

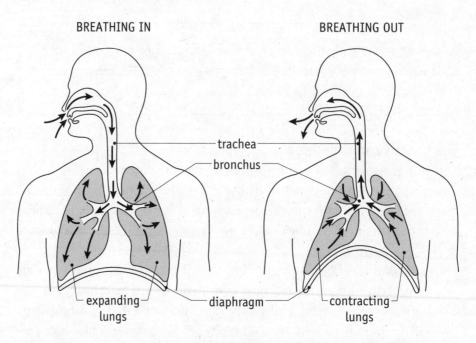

BREATHING IN   BREATHING OUT

trachea
bronchus

expanding   diaphragm   contracting
lungs   lungs

figure 10 **How Breathing Works**

the body, with the final emissive act of the "masculine" energy stream—the out-breath. These two breaths mark the beginning and end of the sacred breathing cycle that is vital to life.

The Effects of Disturbed Breathing

Unless we suffer from a respiratory disorder, we tend not to think about breathing. It is automatic, under the control of the autonomic nervous system. As with the other systems of the body, we do not have to send a message to our breathing apparatus to keep going because it is a function of the coordinated living body. However, in any group of people, there are breathing habits that range from the highly efficient to the dangerously inefficient, with the latter having long-term health implications.

When we are upset, our breathing rate and heartbeat increase due to the secretion of adrenaline. By controlling our breathing and calming it, we can regain the balance of mind and emotions. This sends a message to the adrenal glands to stop secreting adrenaline so that breathing and heartbeat are further calmed.

Disturbed breathing also affects the proper movement of the diaphragm. When the diaphragm is inhibited, it upsets normal breathing rhythm. But it can be remedied by the simple act of controlling our breathing.

The Subtle Role of Breathing

The cycle of the breath is the basic, physical function of breathing. But it also carries the subtle life force (in Sanskrit, *prana*; in Chinese, *qi*) to every part of the body via the blood system. This ability of the breath to carry subtle energies means that we are able to take in healing energies from the energy field and through conscious breathing.

The breath of life is so much more than our unconscious breathing in and out. When a newborn baby takes its first breath, it is an affirmation of the role of air as the carrier of oxygen and the life force. Just as the in-breath is a way of taking in, and receiving, what we need, so the out-breath is a signal for energy to escape. Anything that needs to escape, to be released, or to find a way out of the system can do so with the out-breath. When you use the breath in this way—to let go of stress or anxiety, for example—it is helpful to do it with an open mouth, as this reminds you that your conscious out-breath has the function of release.

The next exercise will introduce you to the benefits of breathing more fully and deeply. If you have any form of breathing difficulty, please remember the following proviso: *All exercises in this book that involve conscious breathing should only be carried out under supervision.*

---

exercise 12 **FULL-BREATH BREATHING**

This exercise reeducates your physical body about efficient energy breathing, maximizing available energies for intake and output. It rebalances the whole system and realigns all aspects of your being.

- Sit comfortably with your feet flat on the ground. Notice your breathing. Allow it to become slow, deep, and gentle.

exercise continues >

- Notice what your chest and abdomen are doing. In full-breath breathing, the focus is on the movement of the abdomen, rather than the chest. Put your hands on your abdomen and imagine it is a balloon you are going to fill and then empty.

- As you slowly inhale through the nose, allow your "balloon" to fill by letting your abdomen gently expand. Do not strain.

- Exhale slowly and feel the balloon of your abdomen deflate. Again, do not strain.

- Practice this exercise three times. Note the difference between the in-breath and the out-breath. Note how you feel as you breathe like this.

The next time you see a sleeping baby, notice the way the baby breathes. How different is this from the way you generally breathe? Full-breath breathing is also known as "soft-belly breathing" because it encourages the relaxation of the abdomen and discourages the tense, hard-belly approach to body posture. Breathing and posture affect our mood and attitude. They can easily be trained to affect both in a positive way. The soft-belly posture allows you to breathe deeply and gently so that you are calm and balanced, with your center of gravity below your navel.

Full-breath breathing may also be used as a self-healing activity to improve breathing capacity and rhythm, benefiting the whole physical system.

Relaxation

The next attunement step of conscious relaxation goes hand in hand with conscious breathing. Relaxation relieves tension and stress at all levels, allowing the body energies to flow more freely. The activities of the brain, heart, and lungs are slowed down, calming the mind and emotions. This creates the ideal state for attunement, Distant Healing, and meditation.

The following exercise is a simple, yet thorough, method of relaxing the whole body. In it you send a command to the brain to allow all the muscles to relax, release, and let go. You coordinate this with slow, deep, gentle breathing, which immediately sends positive messages to all the body systems that things are becoming calm and peaceful. Once your body and mind are acquainted with the feeling of relaxation, you will be able to move into relaxation mode at will. This will be an essential element in your attunement procedure.

exercise 13 **FULL-BODY RELAXATION**
You may find it useful to record the exercise or have it read out to you by your working partner.

- Ideally, you should lie on a firm, even surface with a comfortable support for your head and neck.

- Allow your legs to part slightly and move your hands away from the sides of your body. Carry out the full breath three times as in Exercise 12. Breathe slowly, gently, and normally.

- Focus on your hands. Clench them tightly to make a fist with the in-breath, and let them unclench with the out-breath. Remember the feeling of unclenching (relaxing) and letting go as you exhale. Do not clench anything again throughout the rest of this exercise. As you breathe, know that you are breathing in peace and relaxation. Let any anxieties or problems go with the out-breath and breathe them out through the open mouth.

- Bring your focus to the toes of your left foot. Feel them relax, one by one. Use the out-breath to let go, release, and relax. Move slowly over your foot, relaxing the muscles. Let the ankle go.

exercise continues >

- Move up your left leg, relaxing the muscles. Let the knee joint go. Relax the thigh muscles and the muscles of the buttocks.

- Let go across the pelvis. Continue to breathe slowly and gently.

- Focus on your right foot and proceed in the same way. Feel the toes relax, one by one. Move slowly over your right foot, relaxing the muscles; relaxing and letting go. Let the ankle go.

- Move up your right leg, let the knee joint go. Relax the thigh muscles and the muscles of the buttocks. Relax the pelvis again.

- Now move your attention up the front of your body, relaxing the belly and stomach. Let go of the muscles of the chest. Let go of the shoulders.

- Return your attention to the lower back and slowly relax your back muscles, one by one. Remember to use the out-breath to let go and unclench. If you suffer from back pain, make sure you take time to relax all the back muscles. Pay attention to the muscles across the top of your back and shoulders, where tension tends to gather. Relax and let go.

- Relax the left shoulder and move down the left arm. Let the elbow joint go. Move down the forearm, relaxing and letting go. Let the wrist relax.

- Relax the palm, thumb, and fingers, one by one.

- Return to the right shoulder. Relax it and move down the right arm. Let the elbow joint go. Move down the forearm, relaxing and letting go. Let the wrist relax.

exercise continues >

- Relax the right hand, letting go of your thumb and fingers one by one. Relax the whole shoulder girdle.

- Now move up the back of your neck, very slowly, relaxing and letting go. Let your attention come up the back of your head and over the top of the scalp, relaxing and letting go of all the tiny muscles.

- Imagine a caring hand smoothing your forehead. Relax the eyes, the cheeks, the mouth, the jaw.

- Continue to breathe slowly, gently, and normally. Scan your body to see if any part has tensed up again. If it has, relax it, enjoying the feeling of total relaxation. At this point, you can remain mentally alert or allow yourself to drift off into sleep.

When you repeat this exercise, try starting the relaxation at the top of your body, making your way down to the toes, using the same techniques. See which order is most comfortable for you. You may find that you need to use a different order to suit different times or circumstances. Practice relaxation so that it becomes second nature and you can do it anywhere, in any circumstance, in any position. This exercise facilitates a loving communication with every aspect of your physical form, reestablishing a positive relationship with the body.

Addressing Your Work Space

Distant Healing can be carried out anywhere and at any time, but you will probably carry out most of your practice indoors, perhaps in a dedicated space. Use the following guidance on attuning your work space according to where you wish to practice.

Your work space has an energy field, no matter what its location or size. Just as you need to be attuned to the Source, so does the space. First, pay attention to the space's physical aspects. It should be clean and fresh. Next, clear, balance, and harmonize the room or space, as you did with yourself.

This can be done with smoke, such as incense, using the same technique that Native Americans use when "smudging" with sage or some other herb. The smoke is wafted into all areas of the room. Some healers like to use a light source, such as a candle, or a sound source, such as a bell or the clapping of hands. You can even visualize your work space being cleared and balanced in the same way that you worked on yourself with color. What color of energy does your room need to be filled with? Make a note and see if this color changes the next time you need to work there. Perhaps you have a special ritual, prayer, chant, or song. This is fine. Your intention guides the process. The next exercise, using an incense stick, is a suggestion along these lines that you can adapt in any way you wish. Note what the various actions are for.

---

exercise 14 **PREPARING AND DEDICATING THE WORK SPACE**
Use some of the earlier procedures in this book to calm and relax yourself. When you are ready, put your mind on your heart center (in the middle of your chest). Take a few moments to breathe in and out of this center. Light an incense stick. Dedicate the light and smoke to the Light of healing. Ask for protection as you open yourself to be a channel for healing energies. Ask for help to be as pure a channel as possible.

• Ask that the smoke be used to clear, balance, and harmonize your space.

• Remain focused as you hold the incense stick. Intuitively face a certain direction of the space. Move in a circle from where you are standing, allowing the smoke to spread out into the space before you. Take your time and do not hurry this procedure. Use your other hand to help waft the smoke over the furniture, especially any chairs, and into any corners.

exercise continues >

- If you find that you need to move in an anticlockwise direction, you are clearing the energies of the space. If you find that you need to move in a sunwise (clockwise) direction, you are filling the space with new energies and raising the energy level.

- As you move around, you might like to ask that the space be cleared of all energies that are not compatible with healing. Ask that the space be filled with the energies of healing: the energies of peace, love, and light. Ask for a blessing on the space and all who enter it, or give a blessing yourself.

- If you work in a building shared by others, ask for a blessing on the room, the building, and all who work (and live) in it.

- Wait for an intuitive signal that the job of clearing and dedicating the space has been completed.

There is plenty of scope here for your favorite methods of clearing a space, but check intuitively if they feel right for the task of Distant Healing, which is to follow. Any room or space, whether inside or outside, is conscious; attunement raises this consciousness by accelerating the vibrations of the field, just as it raises the vibrations of your own energy field.

Much of the energetic activity of attunement occurs on a subtle level, involving energies that vibrate faster than the speed of light. Recall that you have a subtle energy system designed to process these energies—the energies of healing and the other subtle energies that are vital to our lives as physical, emotional, mental, and spiritual beings.

Attunement to the Source of Healing Energies

Once you have attuned your Distant Healing space, you can move to the final step in your attunement. Attunement is very much based on your conscious intention, and you may well find that your work on the space has brought you to a place of total quiet focus, especially if you have carried it out with your mind focused on your heart center. Practice Exercise 1: Attunement (page 17) again to compare your deeper sense of attunement with your initial experience in Chapter 1.

Remember that attunement, with your focus on the heart center, is the key element in all your Distant Healing work. If you wish to use it as a form of meditation, practice in the morning and evening. Start with a few minutes each session, gently building up to half an hour over a period of weeks.

Having set up the first side of that powerful energetic structure—the Healing Triangle—you are now ready to work.

Positive Attitudes Mean Good Preparation

Distant Healing can be applied to people, animals, plants, a landscape, and situations. From a healing point of view, situations have moved to the top of the list in terms of priority. This does not mean, however, that individuals no longer matter; far from it. But we are all living in a time when the situations and circumstances in which individuals find themselves range from the dangerous, tragic, and painful to the extremely stressful, confrontational, and life-threatening, to name but a few. Our time calls for new forms of action and commitment. When people feel disempowered and under threat, they become victims of fear. Some fear turns to violent and destructive action; some to apathy and cynicism. The life situations that daily appear on our screens and radios and in our news media are the giant wounds that need urgent healing. Those "on the ground," facing up to or living with these wounds, need more help than they will ever physically get.

This is where Distant Healing comes in. I told you the story about the young pregnant woman to illustrate how healing energies address the whole energetic situation that surrounds someone. Not only were the young woman and her baby helped, but also the behavior and mind-sets of others in her life were altered for the better. Now imagine these possibilities enlarged to whatever scale they may be vitally needed.

From now on, every time you are confronted with some fearful vision or some dreadful news, realize that you are far from powerless to do something. But positive thinking alone is not enough. Positive thinking may help *you* to cope, but it won't make much difference to the violence or suffering that is going on at some distance from you. Because of Oneness, in some way, it is happening to all of us.

There is a biblical story about the first humans, Eve and Adam, that illustrates the necessity of alignment and attunement when practicing Distant Healing. They were having fun, discovering the abundance of the primeval Garden of Eden, when the Holy One called out, "Where are you?" This is often taken to mean that Eve and Adam were hiding—as if the One who made everything, including them and the Garden, did not know where they were! Another level of meaning, taught by New Mexico rabbi Gershon Winkler, is that the Holy One was actually asking them, "Where are *you?* Where is your *consciousness* now? Is it confined to awareness of your wonderful bodies and the physical world around you, or is it also aligned with Oneness?" This deeper meaning is a good reminder about where we need to be whenever we contemplate Distant Healing.

Now fully prepared, in the next chapter, we will make a start as Distant Healers. Later, we will look at the benefits of sharing the work with others in the form of a Distant Healing group.

Chapter 5

Baseline Practice

Creating a Healing List

We begin with the fundamental practice of Distant Healing that you will be able to adapt to the various calls that come your way. You will need to start a Distant Healing book in which you will note all the persons, animals, landscapes, situations, and so on to which you are going to send healing. This is your Distant Healing list. If someone has been referred to you, make a note of the date and ask the referrer to keep in touch and let you know at regular intervals how the person concerned is getting on.

When working with something like a landscape or a situation, note when you begin work and do your own monitoring. You may also like to compile a "scrapbook" of relevant press cuttings of events and situations and other illustrated materials. Gradually, your Distant Healing book will begin to reveal the pattern of your work.

Your preparations for Distant Healing foster at-oneness and a positive mind-set. The positive mind-set requires you to be happy in your work, to look forward to it, while not being attached to an outcome. Distant Healing is a way of developing and practicing unconditional love, the true gift of the heart. This unconditional attitude implies nonattachment to, yet total empathy with, the subject and those who may be asking for your help.

Distant Healing encourages you to approach the work so that each case has your unconditional positive regard and each case is of equal value.

The energetic law of attraction means that once you have indicated to the Source that you are available to work, people will seek your help, and situations will present themselves. This happens when the time is right for your paths to cross; this is especially true in the case of a person or an animal. The moment of meeting has been arranged at a soul level with the agreement of all concerned. It is a moment of sacred synchronicity. A telephone call from the patient is particularly effective, because it carries the vibration of the caller to you. This vibration will be activated later when you come across that person's name, or the name of the third party, on your list.

How the Subject Can Help

When people ask for your help, either for themselves or for a third party, asking them to give you a progress report encourages them to take responsibility for their requests. Asking patients to join in can further empower them while also helping you. Ideally, the patient joins in at the same time as the healing is being sent, though this is not crucial. (As explained earlier, the energies travel outside of the space-time continuum.) Invite patients to sit or lie quietly at the time you will be sending healing to them. Ask them to relax, breathe normally, and visualize a sphere of protective light around them. They should remain like this for fifteen minutes if possible.

When subjects are able to join you in this way, they frequently sense the energies in all kinds of ways and are able to give you feedback about their experience. This may or may not coincide with your experience of their healing. A subject's feedback is always interesting, and it demonstrates the many wonderful ways in which healing energy manifests.

The Unconditional Intention

Because energy follows thought, it travels at the level of that thought. This energy law means that the Distant Healer should pay attention to the way the request for help is made, taking care to avoid being influenced by this principle. For example, the requester tells you that he has a friend who has been diagnosed with bronchitis, which was caused by smoking and says, "You should send some extra healing in case he develops lung cancer, and he probably needs help to give up his addiction to nicotine as well." In such cases, you will need to listen dispassionately to the request without taking on the statements and feelings around it. In your response to this request, take care to say that your way of working is to send healing to the person not the condition, without sounding as if you are making a judgment about the requester.

All you need is the name of the subject and to know whether he or she has agreed to accept Distant Healing help. These precautions are necessary because the initial impulse of love (the urge to ask for help) has become distorted by the mind-based opinions of the requester. When this happens, the energy, traveling at the level of such thoughts, may be unwanted, unnecessary, or ineffective. This is why the Distant Healer does not attempt to direct the healing to a certain aspect or level of a person, though this may well occur during the healing process. In the same way, the unconditional nature of the work means that it cannot involve any kind of judgment or moral attitude toward the requester or possible third-party subject.

The Two Methods of Baseline Practice

Every time you go to work as a Distant Healer, have your list ready, itemizing who and what you wish to send out to. Your list should not be so long that you get tired or lose focus. Start with six to ten cases and a session of around half an hour. Gradually build your list until you find the optimum number for a fully effective and comfortable session. A long list may mean more than one session a week. However long or short your list, part of Distant Healing is to always include requests for peace and healing for the planet and the Earth family, and all the other beings that dwell here with us.

There are two methods of baseline practice. In the first, you attune, receive the Light, and send that healing energy out to the subject. In the second, you attune, receive the Light, and put that healing energy in front of you to form a "pool" or "column." The subject is then immersed in the healing energy pool or column. Through practicing both these methods, you will be fully prepared to work both ways with a group and to do the more advanced work in Part Two.

exercise 15 **SENDING OUT THE HEALING LIGHT**

- Make sure the phone is disconnected and that you will not be disturbed. Attune yourself and your work space as outlined in the previous chapters.

- You may wish to light a candle as a symbol of the Light of the Source. If so, dedicate it to the work and to any helpers you might have in the spiritual realms. Give thanks that you have been given the opportunity to send out healing Light.

- Bring your focus to your heart center. As you inhale, visualize this center filling with the Light. With the next breath, the Light fills your chest.

- As you look over your list, ask for the Light to be sent out to each subject as you mention them one by one. You can say aloud or in your mind, "I ask for healing to be sent to (name)." Carefully work through your list. Take your time, pausing if necessary. Pausing simply means that you are in tune with what is happening energetically.

- When you reach the end of your list, give thanks.

- Rest assured that all those on your list have received the healing they need. Sit quietly with your experience.

- When you have completed your work, blow out the candle. When you blow out the candle, you can send out the light of the candle. Pause for a moment before blowing it out and see if you intuitively feel where the light needs to go. This is usually the first place

exercise continues >

that comes to mind and could be a person, a strife-ridden place, an environment under threat, and so forth. As you blow out the candle, say, "I send the Light out to . . . "

- Once you have closed your session, you have handed over the list to higher powers. It is time to stop thinking about your cases.

In the early stages of practice, alternate the first basic technique of sending out the Light (as in Exercise 15) with the second basic technique of creating the Light pool or circle, as described in the next exercise.

exercise 16 **CREATING THE LIGHT POOL**

- Make sure the phone is disconnected and that you will not be disturbed. Attune yourself and your work space as outlined in the previous chapters.

- You may wish to light a candle as a symbol of the Light of the Source. If so, dedicate it to the work and to any helpers you might have in the spiritual realms. Give thanks that you have been given the opportunity to help others through the Light of Distant Healing.

- Bring your focus to your heart center. As you inhale, visualize this center filling with Light. With the next breath, the Light fills your chest.

- Now see this Light extending from you to a place in front of you, making an energy pool or circle.

- As you look over your list, ask for those on it to be put in the

exercise continues >

Light, mentioning them one by one. You can say aloud or in your mind, "I ask for healing for (name)." Carefully work through your list. Take your time, pausing if necessary. Pausing simply means that you are in tune with what is happening energetically.

- When you reach the end of your list, give thanks.

- Visualize that all those on the list have been gathered into the Light pool or circle, where they will receive the healing they need. Sit quietly with your experience.

- When you have completed your work, blow out the candle. When you blow out the candle, you can send out the light of the candle. Pause for a moment before blowing it out and see if you intuitively feel where the light needs to go. This is usually the first place that comes to mind. As you blow out the candle, say, "I send the Light out to . . ."

- Once you have closed your session, you have handed over the list to higher powers. It is time to stop thinking about your cases.

Baseline Practice: The Closing-Down Procedure

Your baseline practice (as set out in Exercises 15 and 16) is complete only when you have carried out the essential Closing-Down Procedure described below.

If you wish to follow a Distant Healing session with some other spiritual practice, such as meditation, you are in the ideal state to do this. If not, realize that the work has opened your energy centers more than is needed for everyday functioning. In other words, you no longer need to be open to that level of energy flow. You now need to carry out the following Closing-Down Procedure to realign your centers and protect your energy field. This is particularly necessary if you are going to mix with other people in any way, such as going to the supermarket, for you would otherwise be too open to their energies.

When your Distant Healing session is in the evening, the Closing-Down Procedure also ensures sound sleep. "Closing down" means returning your subtle energy system to everyday functioning; it is linked to closing your working sessions. It does not, however, mean fully closing the energy centers or shutting down any of the body systems.

Carrying out the Closing-Down Procedure after each session of work will eventually become second nature. You can use it to return your subtle energy system to everyday functioning at other times, too. Even having a conversation or reading a book about spiritual matters can open your centers. But remember that the centers should never be forcibly closed.

During the day, most people absorb a variety of energies from other people, from places they visit, and from the things they do. Sensitive people, like healers and other therapists, tend to absorb even more into their energy fields. Some of these energies are incompatible with your own, and you sense them through feelings of heaviness, restlessness, even depression. Realize that they are not *your* feelings; take appropriate steps to deal with them.

The first Closing-Down exercise clears incompatible energies. This is the same as Exercise 10 in Chapter 4. I repeat it here so that you don't have to turn back. Recall that this exercise uses the clearing energy of silver light.

The standing stance described in the following two exercises has important beneficial effects. It aligns the centers, facilitates grounding, and frees the energy circuits to flow appropriately.

---

exercise 10 (cont. from page 41) **CLEARING THE ENERGY FIELD**

- Stand, or sit if necessary, with your feet shoulder-width apart and your arms hanging loosely by your sides. Gently flex the knees and allow your body to relax. Use your breath to aid with relaxation and attunement.

exercise continues >

- Take a moment to be aware of any heavy energy in your body and energy field, noting where it seems to have accumulated. (It is worth making a note of this observation in your journal every time you do this exercise to see if there is a pattern.)

- Now visualize yourself under a shower or gentle waterfall of silver light. Let this light pour over you, through you, and out into your surrounding field, especially to any place where you sensed an accumulation of heavy energy. Allow the light to exit through your hands and feet and every body orifice (Figure 8, page 42).

- Notice the color of the light that moves in to fill the space that you have cleared. Your awareness of this color will confirm that the clearing is taking place. You might sense this in a number of ways. If you feel you are sensing nothing (it is your mind saying you can't), carry out this important exercise as if you can sense something.

- Note the sensations of clearing and the sensations of being cleansed.

Next, we bring the centers from being wide open back to everyday functioning. First, check that you remember the location of each of the seven centers and their colors. If necessary, refer to Figure 7 (page 36).

exercise 17 **REGULATING THE ENERGY CENTERS**
For the purpose of this exercise, visualize your centers as flowers with petals that are able to close up but not shut tightly. The exercise is carried out by visualizing the "flowers" of each center gently

exercise continues >

closing up a little. Your intention is to bring them to everyday functioning. See the colors as light.

- Stand relaxed with your knees gently flexed, as in Exercise 10. Start at the crown center, which is violet. Visualize it closing up a little.

- Move your awareness to the brow center—color indigo/royal blue. Close it up a little.

- Move to the throat center—color sky-blue. Close it up a little.

- Move to the heart center—color green. Close it up a little.

- Move to the solar plexus center—color golden yellow. Close it up a little.

- Move to the sacral center—color orange. Close it up a little.

- Move to the base center—color glowing red. Close it up a little.

- Now notice the first color that comes to mind. This is the color of energy that will keep your system in place. Surround yourself with a sphere of this light.

This is also a grounding process. Note the direction of activity—from the highest vibration of the crown center to that closest to the Earth at the base center.

The final part of the Closing-Down Procedure keeps your energy field strong and protects you by not allowing entry of incompatible energies.

exercise 18 **THE SPHERE OF PROTECTION**

figure 11 **The Sphere of Protection**

• Still standing relaxed and breathing naturally, knees gently flexed, surround the sphere of colored light (as in Exercise 17) with a sphere of golden light. See the golden sphere sparkle and gleam. This will tell you about its energy of strength and protection. Spend a moment of awareness before moving from your place.

You can also use the Sphere of Protection whenever you wish to protect or maintain the integrity of your energy field, such as when

exercise continues >

traveling, going shopping, being with crowds, or being with individuals or in situations where the energies seem incompatible with your own. You can also use it at the end of the day before sleep.

Your Complete Baseline Practice

The two Distant Healing practices and the Closing-Down Procedure in this chapter are your complete baseline practice. All the other practices of Distant Healing, including the advanced ones, derive from this simple format. This focused work brings with it all the benefits of meditation, such as reduced blood pressure, a stronger immune system, mental clarity, emotional stability, and communication with your Higher Self. These are not reasons for doing Distant Healing, but they are its positive and welcome by-products. Similarly, the Closing-Down Procedure reminds you that part of the work is to look after yourself and your energy field.

Chapter 6

Baseline Practice—
The Healing Circle

The Group Experience

However much we might enjoy working solo, in Distant Healing, we are always aware that we are actually working with at least one other person. This person links us to society and the global family. Humans thrive in community. Therefore, if it is possible, I recommend that you join with another or others on a regular basis to do Distant Healing as a group. This not only provides you with the benefits of company and friendship; you will also have a forum for learning and feedback, as well as the experience of building, and being part of, a group energy. This energy is different from that which you experience when working alone, and it will provide further valuable experience as a Distant Healer.

I hope there will come a time when Distant Healing groups are set up all over the world, in every town and in every country. The energy of a like-minded group is particularly effective in creating favorable conditions for Distant Healing. The Distant Healing Circle provides an opportunity to do service for the community and the wider world, and the basics of the work can be learned almost right away. The format discussed in this chapter is a suggested guideline that can be adapted according to numbers and preferences.

You will need a group leader/facilitator each time you meet; every member should take a turn at leading or facilitating the group. As in the two baseline exercises for individual work (see Chapter 5), the group can practice the exercises in this chapter as follows: Each person brings either a list of requests for healing or a list of those who have intuitively come to mind. The length of the list will be dictated by the time you have together. A list of about ten per person should be enough.

---

exercise 19 THE DISTANT HEALING CIRCLE—SENDING OUT THE HEALING LIGHT

Disconnect all telephones. Arrange the chairs in a circle with a small table in the center with a candle and some matches. Members might like to add items symbolizing healing and so on. When possible, the group should sit with male next to female and experienced next to inexperienced. By alternating genders and experience levels, the energies of the circle are easier to balance.

The chosen leader should open the meeting with a welcome, help the group to attune, and then facilitate the Distant Healing. Make sure that everyone has his or her list of people, animals, situations, and so on. The group members sit in a circle with feet flat on the floor and the hands palms up on their thighs or in their laps without linking. The leader instructs the group as follows:

- "Take six breaths to calm and relax your body, letting go of any worries or anxieties with your out-breath through the open mouth. When you feel attuned, close your mouth and breathe normally.

- "Check that your body is relaxed, including the back of your neck, shoulders, and pelvis. Close your eyes and allow the calm silence to settle on our Circle."

exercise continues >

- The leader lights the candle and dedicates the Light to the work of the Circle, asking for protection and soul guidance.

- The leader continues: "The light of the candle is the Light of the Source of healing. Breathe it into the heart center. Allow the Light to fill your chest.

- "Now pass the energy in your heart center to the person on your left so that you are all linked together." Intuitively, you may have to wait a moment to gather your heart energy before you can pass it on. The leader should be aware of everyone's need to gather his or her energies and allow enough time for group linking, for this is the foundation of the Circle. With practice, it is possible to sense when energetic linking is complete.

- The leader expresses the purpose of the meeting and gives thanks, on behalf of the group, for the opportunity to be of service.

- The leader begins to read out his or her list, asking for healing Light to be sent to each person named. A simple form of this could be, "I ask for healing to be sent to (name)." The leader indicates that the list is complete with a verbal signal, such as "Thank you."

- The person on the leader's left then reads out his or her list and repeats the concluding signal. Follow this procedure until everyone has read out his or her list.

- With your eyes closed, you can create an inner "screen" (just above the brow) on which you may be able to "see" the people named. It is important to know that your intention, motivated by love, has enabled the light of healing to be sent to them.

exercise continues >

- As you sit together in the silence, the leader gives time for quiet reflection.

- After a short break, the group can discuss the work of the Circle and share experiences and queries to consolidate learning.

- The work may be followed by another spiritual activity, such as meditating, giving a reading, or listening to music.

- Finally, the leader closes the Healing Circle. As the candle is blown out, the Light can be sent out to where it is needed, as when working alone—to a strife-ridden place, an environment under threat, and so on.

- Before closing the meeting, the group should carry out the Closing-Down Procedure, which can be led by the chosen leader.

The reflection time can be used to make notes or to illustrate the experience in some way. This allows group members to log their experience and learning, chart the energies they have been working with, and ground the experience. It gives the mind time to absorb what has happened, which is one of the building blocks of group work.

Members can also devise activities for coming together as a group. These should help them leave behind the life they lead outside the meeting place. I have suggested a format above, but there can be different types of group activity. For example, the group leader for a particular meeting could suggest the topic for group activity, such as a local, national, or global crisis. This utilizes the group's ability to channel energy to such situations, rather than to the individual lists.

The group can also alternate sending out the Light with the second baseline technique for group work—creating the Light column.

exercise 20 **THE DISTANT HEALING CIRCLE—
CREATING THE LIGHT COLUMN**

Disconnect all telephones. Arrange the chairs in a circle with a small table in the center with a candle and some matches. Members might like to place items on the table that symbolize healing. When possible, the group should sit with male next to female and experienced next to inexperienced. By alternating genders and experience levels, the energies of the circle are easier to balance.

The chosen leader should open the meeting with a welcome, help the group to attune, and then facilitate the Distant Healing. Make sure that everyone has his or her list of people, animals, situations, and so on.

- The group members sit in a circle with feet flat on the floor and the hands palms up on their thighs or in their laps without linking. The leader instructs the group as follows:

- "Take six breaths to calm and relax your body, letting go of any worries or anxieties with your out-breath through the open mouth. When you feel attuned, close your mouth and breathe normally.

- "Check that your body is relaxed, including the back of your neck, shoulders, and pelvis. Close your eyes and allow the calm silence to settle on our Circle."

- The leader lights the candle and dedicates the Light to the work of the Circle, asking for protection and soul guidance.

- The leader continues: "The light of the candle is the Light of the Source of healing. Breathe it into the heart center. Allow the Light to fill your chest."

exercise continues >

figure 12 **The Distant Healing Circle—Creating the Light Column**

- "Now pass the energy in your heart center to the person on your left so that you are all linked together." Intuitively, you may have to wait a moment to gather your heart energy before you can pass it on. The leader should be aware of this and allow enough time for group linking, for this is the foundation of the Circle. With practice, it is possible to sense when energetic linking is complete.

- The leader expresses the purpose of the meeting and gives thanks, on behalf of the group, for the opportunity to be of service.

- The leader continues: "As you are aware of the Light in the heart center, in your mind's eye, see this Light extending from you to

exercise continues >

the center of the Circle." In this way, every member helps build a central column of Light, the Light of healing.

- The leader begins to read out his or her first list, asking for healing for each person named, knowing that they will be put or held in the Light. A simple form of this could be, "I ask for healing for (name)." The leader indicates that the list is complete with a verbal signal, such as "Thank you."

- The person on the leader's left then reads out his or her list and repeats the concluding signal. Follow this procedure until everyone has read out his or her list.

- By watching your inner "screen" (above the brow), you may be able to "see" the people named, or you may not. It is important to know that your intention, motivated by love, has put them in the Light of healing.

- As you sit together in the silence, retain your awareness of the Light. See if your inner screen shows you what is happening to the Light.

- The leader gives time for quiet reflection.

- After a short break, the group can discuss the work of the Circle and share experiences and queries to consolidate learning.

- The work may be followed by another spiritual activity, such as meditating, giving a reading, or listening to music.

- Finally, the leader closes the Healing Circle. As the candle is blown out, the Light can be sent out to where it is needed, as when working alone.

- Before closing the meeting, the group should carry out the Closing-Down Procedure, which can be led by the chosen leader.

As in Exercise 19, reflection time can be used to make notes or to illustrate the experience in some way. This allows group members to log their experience and learning, chart the energies with which they have been working, and ground the experience. It gives the mind time to absorb what has happened, which is one of the building blocks of group work.

Members can also devise activities for coming together as a group. These should help them leave behind the life they lead outside the meeting place. I have suggested a format above, but there can be different types of group activity. For example, the group leader for a particular meeting could suggest the topic for group activity, such as a local, national, or global crisis. This utilizes the group's ability to channel energy to such situations, rather than to the individual lists.

Moving on to Part Two

When you and your Distant Healing Circle feel confident with your practice so far, you are ready to move forward with the topics in Part Two.

Beginning with important information about the body's subtle energy circuits and the energy centers, Part Two looks at how we are affected by our Distant Healing work and the effects of negative energies in general. This is followed by the advanced techniques for solo and group work. In addition to strengthening your traditional practice with persons and animals, your work with Part Two will equip you to make a valuable contribution to global healing.

part two

Chapter 7

The Energy Circuits of the Body

The Polarity Channels of the Etheric Body

On each side of the central channel of the etheric body, and connected to it, are two other channels that extend from the base to the brow centers. The circulation of energy in these two channels creates a balance between the inflow and the outflow of subtle energies throughout the system, including each of the centers.

The polarities of energy have historically been referred to as masculine and feminine, based on the relative roles of male and female in procreation, but these terms describe qualities of energy flow, not aspects of gender. Everyone has both channels and both energies. The emissive right side of the field processes energies that are outgoing. The receptive left side processes energies that are incoming.

For emotional and mental health, as well as physical well-being, the energies of the two polarities should be in a state of balance; however, it is easy for them to get out of balance. Our mental and emotional state, our thoughts and behavior, have an instant effect on this balance. For example, when we are not assertive enough in a given situation, so that we allow ourselves to be disempowered, the emissive energies are not being used when they need to be. The polarities are either thrown out of balance or

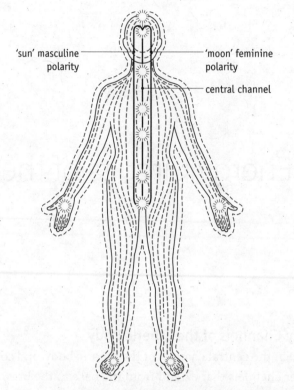

'sun' masculine
polarity

'moon' feminine
polarity

central channel

figure 13 **The Polarity Channels of the Etheric Body**

their imbalance has caused us to be unable to stand up for ourselves. We then experience feelings such as anger, frustration, or self-disgust, which serve as warning signals that our energies are out of balance. If this goes on for too long, so that one energy stream is unused or underdeveloped, the other will try to compensate by dominating the system and all its activities. This is self-defeating because it nurtures the initial weakness.

Experience will tell you when your healing work is involved in restoring polarity balance (see also Exercise 23: Checking Polarity Balance, page 86).

The Template for the Body

The template for the formation, development, and composition of the physical body is found in the etheric body. Thus, the symmetry of the body is derived from the symmetry of the etheric, with its central channel and network of energy centers. The body's ability to process the flow of substances to and from its organs is derived from the flow of energies in the etheric channels. The seven main energy centers are the structures from which the seven endocrine glands are derived. Other physical organs originate in other large energy centers. The nervous system is derived from the etheric energy channels, and the vascular (blood) system from the flow of energies within the etheric network. The fact that we can absorb subtle energies through the skin is due to the presence of tiny energy centers throughout the surface of the etheric body. These foundations of the physical body have a direct bearing on how and whether healing energies flow into the body from a spiritual level.

Throughout the existence of the body, the etheric level conveys the life force, which is essential to the animation of all physical forms, along with vitalizing energies that enter via the sacral and solar plexus centers. In this way, the etheric level is the energetic support system for physical life. This gateway between the physical and the nonphysical is the entry point where the Higher Self and its subtle energies can take a physical form.

We Are Beings of Light

It is essential to realize that we are, first and foremost, conscious beings of Light, manifestations of the Oneness. The Light being, or soul, originates its own subtle aspects (mental, emotional, and etheric) that support and make possible the life of the physical. We are then able to develop an individual personality consciousness from the time of conception onward.

As we have all experienced, the problem with our personality consciousness is that it can easily convince us that *it* is the real us. It is only pressure from our Higher Self, or soul, that encourages us to consider that we have a far greater consciousness. All of this does mean, however, that when the personality becomes unconscious, as it does during sleep and at death, the Higher Self withdraws from the physical, and we move into consciousness at some subtle level.

The Skeleton and Its Subtle Energies

For the body to act as the soul's traveling vehicle, it needs a structure that will provide a strong, rigid, yet movable base. This is the physical role of the skeleton. The symmetrical structure of the skeleton has a central flexible *figure 14* **The Skeletal Energy Circuits**

column, the spine, which protects the central nervous system. The spine is topped by the skull, which houses and protects the brain—the "computer" of all the body systems. The spine supports the two girdles of the shoulders and pelvis, from which hang the bones of the arms and legs. The rib cage, emanating from the spine and joined in front by the breast bone, houses and protects the heart, lungs, stomach, liver, and associated organs.

Etheric consciousness is aware of the energetic state of the bones through the subtle energy circuits of the skeleton. In Figure 14, these energy circuits are indicated in black for clarity, but they should be visualized as fine lines of light. The bones carry information about where a person is on his or her life journey. They are also our link with the mineral kingdom and its Earth memory.

Since your work may well involve the skeletal energy circuits, the following exercises will introduce you to them. You will need a partner and, if possible, a healing couch or a means of working with your partner lying down. There is also an exercise with your partner sitting on a chair.

exercise 21 **SENSING THE SKELETAL ENERGY CIRCUITS**

Look again at the diagram of the skeleton in Figure 14. Your intention in this exercise is to make contact with the skeletal energy circuits, with your palm centers acting as scanning sensors. You will hold your hands, palms down, two to four inches above your partner's body. The subtle energies of the skeleton radiate beyond the physical body. Thus it is perfectly possible to scan the spine from above. In hands-on healing, this fact enables the healer to work with patients who are unable to lie on their stomachs in prone position.

You will first scan down the primary circuit of the spine, then down the secondary circuits of one side—the shoulder girdle and the arm, the pelvis and the leg. You will then scan down the secondary circuits of the other side, with the spine as the starting point of each secondary circuit. Your partner should lie on his or her back, relaxing and breathing normally. At all times, follow the form of the skeleton. To get used to the procedure, you may find it helpful to have a practice run. Note your sensations at each part of the scanning and sensing.

• Stand by your partner's head and hold both palms about two to four inches away from the top of the skull. Keep a small gap between your two hands. Move your hands slowly over the skull and down over the face toward the neck to sense where the spine links with the skull. This is where your primary scan of the spine

exercise continues >

begins. With your hands two to four inches above the front of the body, move your hands slowly from the neck, following the line of the spine, until you reach its base at the coccyx. Leave one hand here while you extend the other back to the top of the spine. As you stand with your arms extended, see if you can sense the energy of the spine between your two palms.

- To move down the left side of your partner's body, put both palms opposite the base of the neck, keeping a slight gap between them as before. Move them slowly to the top of the left shoulder. Continue slowly down the arm, from joint to joint, until you are able to move out over the hand and the bones of the fingers. Leave one hand here while you extend the other to the top of the left shoulder. Again, see if you can sense the energy of the left arm between your palms.

- Now scan the left leg. Put your hands opposite the base of the spine. Move them slowly across the pelvis to the left hip. Continue slowly down the left leg, from joint to joint, until you are able to move out over the bones of the toes. Leave one hand there while you extend the other back to the hip. See if you can sense the energy of the left leg.

- Scan down the right side of your partner's skeleton in the same way, beginning where the shoulder girdle meets the spine.

- When you have completed your scan of the energy circuits of the skeleton, discuss your impressions with your partner. Change roles. Finally, compare notes with each other.

If you would prefer to work with your partner sitting on a chair, try the next exercise. Read through Exercise 21 first so that you are acquainted with its method and purpose.

exercise 22 **SENSING THE SKELETAL ENERGY CIRCUITS—
PARTNER ON A CHAIR**

• Your partner should sit with feet flat on the ground with legs
uncrossed and hands resting on thighs. His or her palms may be
up or down. You and your partner should relax and breathe normally. Stand behind your partner with your own palms held two
to four inches from the back of the skull, with a slight gap between
your hands. Move your hands slowly down the back of the skull
toward the neck until you sense where the skull joins the spine.
This is where your primary scan of the spine begins.

• Move your palms slowly down the spine until they are opposite
its base at the coccyx. Leave one hand here while you extend the
other to the top of the spine. As in Exercise 21, see if you can feel
the energy of the spine between your two palms.

• To move down the left side of your partner's body, put both palms
at the back of the neck. Move them slowly across to the top of the
left shoulder. Continue down the left arm, joint by joint, until you
are able to move out over the bones of the fingers. Leave one hand
here while you extend the other to the top of the arm. Sense the
energy of the left arm.

• Now scan the left leg. Standing behind the back, put your palms
opposite the base of the spine. Move them slowly across the pelvis
to the left. Continue down the left leg, joint by joint, until you are
able to move out over the bones of the left foot. Leave one hand
here while you extend the other to the top of the leg. Sense the
energy of the left leg.

exercise continues >

- Scan the right side in the same way. Begin with both palms at the base of the neck to scan the right arm. Return to the base of the spine to scan the right leg.

- When you have completed your scan of the skeletal energy circuits, discuss your findings with your partner. Change roles. Finally, compare notes with each other.

The symmetry of the skeleton and its energy circuits reflect the polarity energy channels in the etheric, as shown in Figures 13 (page 80) and 14 (page 82). This symmetry facilitates the balance of energy flow in the skeleton, muscles, and their skeletal attachments. This means that the system seeks to ensure the proper movement of the limbs and their joints, as well as the efficient mobility of the whole structure.

From a Distant Healing point of view, the energy circuits also offer a way in for those energies that are needed to bring balance to a person's being at every level. You may find, therefore, that in some aspect of your work, you are working to restore polarity balance. The next exercise will familiarize you with this procedure.

exercise 23 **CHECKING POLARITY BALANCE**

In this exercise, you will use the soles of the feet, as well as the tops of the shoulders, to sense the energetic polarity balance of the skeleton.

- Your partner should lie on the healing couch or on the ground. Position yourself by your partner's feet with your palms two to four inches away from his or her soles. Relax and breathe normally. See if you can sense the energies emanating from your partner's feet. Do both feet feel the same?

exercise continues >

- Do you sense energy leaving your palms? If so, this is to restore energetic balance. Once this is done, both feet will feel the same energetically.

- What is your partner aware of?

- Change roles and compare notes.

- On another day, position yourself at your partner's head. Hold your palms near the tops of your partner's shoulders. Repeat the above procedures. What do you sense, and what is your partner aware of?

- Again, compare your findings.

exercise 24 **CHECKING POLARITY BALANCE— PARTNER ON A CHAIR**

- This is the same as Exercise 23, but your partner should sit on a chair with legs uncrossed and feet flat on the ground. Your partner's hands should rest on the thighs. You both should relax and breathe normally.

- Squat by your partner's feet and hold your palms near the tops of the feet. See if you can sense the energies emanating from them. Do both feet feel the same?

- Do you sense energy leaving your palms, to bring balance, so that both feet eventually feel the same energetically?

exercise continues >

- What is your partner aware of?

- Change roles and compare notes.

- On another day, stand behind your partner and hold your palms near the tops of your partner's shoulders. Repeat the above procedures. What do you sense, and what is your partner aware of?

- Compare your findings.

You are building a concept of a human being that will form a base for your Distant Healing work. You are beginning to discover that there is much more to you than your physical body. By realizing that your body is the expression of your soul's need to experience physical life, you celebrate your discoveries.

Distant Healing acknowledges the essential *spiritual* nature of all energy. The reality of our body of Light is made possible through its subtle energies. In the next chapter, we will look at the etheric structures that facilitate energetic flow, as well as every aspect of our life and journey. These are the etheric gateways, the subtle energy centers (chakras).

Chapter 8

Etheric Gateways—
The Subtle Energy Centers

The etheric body has some 360 discernible centers, varying in size and function. Distant Healing is particularly concerned with the seven main energy centers, because they act as the gateways and gatekeepers of our life journey, health, and well-being. For this reason, do not attempt to shut off the activity of these centers by "closing" them. Although specific processes are going on in each center, the energetic system operates as a complete and interconnected whole. Through etheric consciousness, each center is aware of all the activities in the energetic system.

The main centers appear as slight depressions in the luminous weblike surface of the etheric body. Each is attached to a central channel, aligned with the spine, which is in turn connected to the network of channels running through the etheric (Figure 7, page 36). When a center is activated, the vortex of light moves out from the surface of the etheric body to project into the energy field. It now appears as a bell- or funnel-shaped structure connected at its narrower end to the central channel. This shape facilitates the gathering or emission of energies.

The etheric effectively acts as the communication vehicle for the soul, enabling the passage of energies from the Higher Self (soul) to the physical and from the physical back to the Higher Self. In doing so, the energy

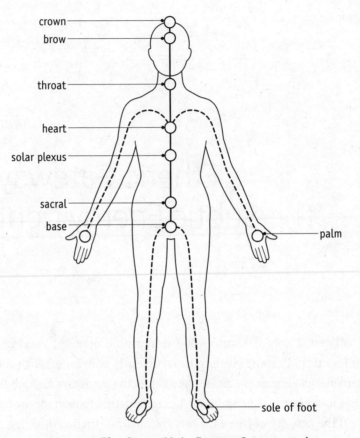

crown
brow
throat
heart
solar plexus
sacral
base
palm
sole of foot

figure 15 **The Seven Main Energy Centers and
the Centers of the Hands and Feet**

centers act as a distribution system for all the energies, including the mental
and emotional energies, generated during life experience. Throughout
these activities, the centers identify subtle energies and, if possible, process
them. But very often a person is not ready to deal with a certain situation,
such as bereavement. In that case, the etheric consciousness stores the relevant energies for processing later.

If unprocessed material is allowed to build up, we begin to receive warning signals from the Higher Self in the form of uncomfortable feelings. If
these warnings are not heeded, the body may become sick so that we are
forced to "listen." Similarly, whenever a person confronts a situation con-
trary to the personal spiritual core, the centers work hard to process the

material. But continued exposure makes this task progressively more difficult, which can exhaust the centers and lead to energetic blockage and subsequent ill-health.

exercise 25 **SENSING THE LOCATION OF THE CENTERS**

You will need a partner for this exercise. Have another look at Figure 15 so that you have a fair idea of where you will be working in this exercise. Take your time with this exercise, pausing between locating each center if you need to.

- Your partner should be seated on a chair with his or her legs and arms uncrossed. (If they remain crossed, there is an energy block at the point of crossover.) Your partner's feet should be flat on the ground, hands resting on the thighs. Your partner should relax and breathe normally.

- Remember to use your breath to help you stay relaxed as your mind starts to collate the subtle energy information you are tracing.

- Stand behind your partner and raise your hands so that your palms are above your partner's crown center with your arms fully extended. Keep a small gap between your hands.

- Slowly lower your arms, allowing your palms to move down toward your partner's crown center until you sense a slight pressure or resistance against your palms. Stop at this point. Notice your sensations.

- This is the edge of the radiation you can sense from the crown center. Notice where the crown center energies extend upward into the energy field.

exercise continues >

- Now you are going to sense the location of the brow center. The energies of the brow center project in front of and behind the center, so you will need to step to one side of your partner while you move your hands to either side of the brow center with your arms extended.

figure 16 **Sensing the Crown Center**

- Slowly bring both your palms in toward the brow center until you feel the slight pressure of its projected energies. Stop at this point and notice where the brow energies extend into the field. Notice any sensations and any differences in sensations.

- Move both hands down to the throat area. Again, extend your arms away from the throat and slowly bring them together to locate the energies of the throat center.

exercise continues >

- Move both hands down to the center of your partner's chest with one hand in front and the other behind with your arms extended. Slowly bring your hands together to locate the heart center.

- Move both hands down to just below your partner's breast bone, above the navel. Keep both arms extended. Slowly bring them together to locate the solar plexus center. You may find that you need to kneel on the ground or use another chair to sit on so that you are comfortable while working with the lower centers. It is important to relax to be fully sensitive.

figure 17 **Sensing the Brow Center**

exercise continues >

- Move both hands just below your partner's navel to locate the sacral center. Keep both arms extended. Slowly bring them together. Again, check your sensations and mentally compare them with those of the other centers.

- Finally, move to the base center. When a person is in a sitting position, the base center energies project upward and downward at an angle of about forty-five degrees. Position yourself so that your palms are held at this angle.

- Proceed in the same way as for the other centers to sense the energies of the base center.

- Relax. After a short break, change roles. Finally, compare notes with your partner.

figure 18 **Sensing the Base Center**

Exercise 25 helped you locate the energies of the centers and showed you how your palm centers are sensitive to them. Now we can look at the life issues that each center is processing. The material presented here is based on my own research over some twenty-five years and has been found to apply to all my patients and to all workshop participants. It is offered as a starting point for your own experiences and awareness.

The seven major centers are located near major organs in the body, some of which are nerve plexuses. As we shall see, each major center deals energetically with specific life issues, such as survival, sexuality, and love. The energies of these processes move in and out of the body via seven endocrine glands (the glands without ducts). In this way, life issues can have an impact on our body, starting at a glandular level and then moving into nearby organs.

Similarly, what happens to our body is conveyed energetically to the relevant center or centers. To give a simple example, a person experiences the loss of a loved one and soon develops a severe cold. This is because the immune system, via the thymus gland, is linked to the heart center, which deals with all issues concerning love. The feelings of grief have manifested as a shock to the immune system, leaving the person vulnerable to infection.

What follows is an outline of the work of the seven centers (or life gateways). We will move in the same direction as the evolutionary force of the center energies: from the base to the crown. Remember, the centers are *etheric* structures. They operate through the relevant endocrine glands, wherever these happen to be physically situated.

The Base Center

Located at the base of the spine, this center is our link with our body, nature, the planet, and the element earth. It processes all issues of a physical nature: how we relate to our body and its physicality; the senses; sensuality; the sex or gender that we are (and remember there are two polarities of male and female, with many variations on those themes); our safety and survival; self-defense and aggression; our relationship to all aspects of the natural world; our relationship to the planet. As you can see, these basic issues are all related to our basic human nature and, energetically, have to be accepted and dealt with.

The base center links with the body via the adrenal glands, which are situated on the top of the kidneys. These glands initiate action and are also concerned with our self-defense—the "fight or flight" response. Interestingly, people, especially children, who have issues around personal safety often have skin problems that affect their hands. If you look at a person when their hands are held by the sides of the body, the hands are aligned with the base center. Thus, base center issues, such as survival, can erupt on the hands as a warning sign that things are not as they should be.

This center is also concerned with the base of the spine, the lower pelvis and related organs, the hips, legs, and feet. It is the keeper of cellular memory for the whole body.

When in a state of balance, the base center vibrates to the color red. Like all center colors, it is seen with subtle vision and is similar, but not identical, to the colors of the physical spectrum. Balance occurs when a person feels safe and secure and has a good relationship with the body and the natural world.

The base center has a special link with the heart and crown centers. This link gives a strong clue about our reality. The base center emphasizes that we are in a physical body in a physical world, but our true nature is love (heart center) and our origins are spiritual (crown center).

The Sacral Center

Located opposite the sacral bones in the spine between the navel and the base center, the sacral center processes all issues of creativity and sexuality. The sacral center is linked with the element of water. This center keeps a subtle energetic record of our development as a child. When a person has experienced childhood trauma, however, the inner child is often found misplaced in either the base or the solar plexus center.

The sacral center is the seat of joy, which is not simply an emotion but also generated energy, telling us that we are in touch with the center's spiritual aspects. Not surprisingly, this joy is often expressed in the form of giggly laughter, especially in children. Being human allows us creative potential (a natural manifestation of our unique divinity). Thus suppression of creativity, or sexuality, creates issues that this center must process.

A useful question when we need to assess how we really feel about something is, Does it give me joy?

The sacral center links with the body via the sex glands (usually the testes in the male or the ovaries in the female). It is concerned with the urogenital organs, the uterus (womb), the kidneys, the lower digestive organs, and the lower back. Males should realize that though they may not have a physical uterus, they do have a sacral center that acts like one. All creations have their beginnings and gestation here.

When in a state of balance, the sacral center vibrates to the color orange. But when our creativity is not expressed, the center moves out of balance and begins to find ways to signal this. The sacral center has a special link with the throat center, where creativity is given expression.

The Solar Plexus Center

Just below the breast bone and the diaphragm and above the navel, the nerve junction known as the solar plexus gives this center its name. The nerves of this plexus radiate out like the rays of the sun and echo their subtle activity pattern in the etheric center. This is where we sense nervous feelings like "butterflies in the stomach," which can affect the diaphragm and thus our breathing. The solar plexus has these physical effects because it links with the body via the islets of Langerhans—the endocrine glands in the pancreas. The energies of the solar plexus center affect the digestive system, the pancreas, the liver and gall bladder, the diaphragm, and the middle back.

The processing of our thoughts, emotions, and feelings, as well as our sense of personal self and personal power, is generated by this center. Here we discover how far life experience has empowered or disempowered us and how we react to people and situations in terms of our sense of self. As we have grown, developed, experienced life, and reacted to the behavior of others, this sense of self has been created by our mind. We should understand, then, that our personality, which embodies our sense of self, is a conditioned being. The unconditioned being that watches over us without any kind of judgment, and that is present at all times, is our Higher Self.

The solar plexus center confronts us with all issues connected to the mind—our thoughts and emotions—especially our conditioned mind-sets. The mind is designed to record and remember, and this process begins in, and continues from, our time in the womb. Because some of our experience will inevitably be negative, we find that not all of our mind's conditioning is conducive to our well-being.

The solar plexus center allows us to store mental and emotional patterns of energy which, because they have not been fully processed, can trigger reactions we would rather not experience. When this occurs, we are in danger of moving into a state of energetic imbalance, and our feelings tell us how uncomfortable this is.

Noticing our triggered reactions is important when considering the solar plexus's link with the brow center. Though the solar plexus center processes mental activity, it has access to the intuitive, or soul, information that comes from the brow. Thus we are able to compare and contrast these two related forms of information. And yet so often we listen to the overriding voice of the mind. For example, have you ever had an idea about something, and it seems like a good idea, but then you start to think it over? You end up changing your mind, only to find later that your first impulse was the best one.

We become conditioned by the rationality of the mind to trust its findings above all else. What we need to remember is that the mind can only work with what it already knows, with what is in the memory bank. Material from the brow is always fresh and often unknown; when the mind is confronted with such material, it tends to advise against using it.

In its balanced state, the solar plexus center vibrates to the color golden yellow.

These first three centers of the system are very much concerned with being physically human and having a human life. The energies moving upward from them next enter the heart center, where they will be assessed to see how much they have been associated with unconditional love.

The Heart Center

Located in the center of the chest (but *not* in the physical heart), the heart center is considered to be the place of the soul. The challenge of the heart center is to express the light of the soul as love, to get its soul message of love through to us, and to deal with all issues about love, and lovelessness, in our life.

The heart center links with the body via the thymus gland. This endocrine gland is quite large when we are very young and tends to diminish in size as we get older. It is partially responsible for the development of the immune system. At a subtle level, this continues to be the heart center's work, in spite of its physically diminished size, so that issues of love and lovelessness affect our immune system throughout life. This is one of the ways that the heart center signals us.

The cardiac and pulmonary nerve plexuses, the heart, lungs, the bronchial tubes, chest, upper back, and arms are all influenced by the heart center. Similarly, information about what happens to these organs passes to other levels of our being via this center.

I mentioned earlier how the energies of the centers can affect the surrounding, or nearby, organs. An interesting and unusual example of this can occur with the hands, because of the energetic link between the heart and base centers. When the arms are held at the sides of the body, the hands are in line with the base center. The hands can manifest conditions triggered by love and/or lovelessness (heart center) and survival (base center). Such conditions include eczema and arthritis.

As can be seen from Figure 15 (page 90), the heart is at the balance point of the seven main centers; thus, balance is one of its important functions. The heart center has to balance the physical energies moving upward toward the brow with the spiritual energies moving downward from the crown. In all cases, the heart center monitors how much the conditioned personality is involved, how much the Higher Self is involved, and the balance between the two. When in a state of balance, it vibrates to the color green, the color of balance. It is not surprising that when we need to revive and refresh ourselves, we go somewhere in nature, unconsciously seeking the energies of the color green.

We are living in a time when this balance point of the centers is also the crisis point in human affairs. If you think back, you will find that some issue around love has been your greatest life challenge so far. It will continue to be so for all people on the planet. Via the heart center, the Higher Self asks, Do you love yourself, and do you love others as the Source? Do you love others because of Oneness, and can you love without judging them? Your heart knows and cannot be fooled.

These questions are also about whether we are at last willing to move from a fear-based to a love-based way of being. The fear-based way keeps us in the solar plexus center, in the grip of the conditioned mind. We know what fear would do; fear trusts power and violence. We have had thousands of years of trying to solve all our problems this way, and we go on with this way in spite of the evidence that it never provides a long-term solution. This is why the challenge of our times is to move our consciousness to the heart center. Then we can ask, What would *Love* do? Love will give an answer to any problem, on any occasion. For when the heart is asked, the soul replies and shows us the way through. We are guided by the Higher Self and its links with the sacred. Love's answer makes everybody happy, and everybody wins.

Distant Healing is a positive response to this challenge from the heart. Where we might have felt helpless in the face of a great need outside ourselves, Distant Healing offers simple ways to bring balance and healing. Love is always dynamic. This is what gives power to the heart energy of compassion, ensuring that our caring response is more than useless pity. Distant Healing can be your way of moving to a love-based way of being.

From the point of balance in the subtle energy system, the next center deals with all aspects of expression and communication. This ranges from expressing who we think we are (our limited and conditioned self-image) to expressing who we really are (our talents and soul mission) to what else is going on in the whole system. It is profoundly influenced by its nearness to the brow center, where intuition (or soul knowledge) is generated.

The Throat Center

Though located in the throat and affecting its related organs, the throat center is the "ear, nose and throat" center, too. It links with the body and these organs via the thyroid gland. As mentioned earlier, the throat has an important energetic link with the sacral central, where everything creative is conceived and gestated.

There is an old wooden grave marker in a cemetery in Arizona on which the epitaph counsels, "Be what you iz, coz if you be what you ain't, then you ain't what you iz." Each center seems to throw out a challenge to us, and that epitaph exactly sums up the challenge of the throat center—to be authentic. Here all issues of expression and communication are processed, as are the different methods we use to express ourselves and communicate with others, with the world, and with the realms of the sacred.

The throat center asks: Do you express who you really are, or only part of yourself, none of yourself, or a distorted aspect of yourself? Do you value truth, or is the lie okay? Untruth accumulates energies like itself. Gradually, whole areas of our being and our life become weighed down with the heavy energies of falsehood and negativity. They have no power to do good, even though this may have been our motive for lying.

In the other centers, it may take time before we are aware of a block in the flow of energies. However, if we suppress the expression of any of the subtle energies, we feel a pain in the throat or the need to cough straight away. I remember as a child being wrongly accused of a misdemeanor and not being allowed to speak up for myself. This created an intense dull pain in my larynx. In this example, not only was expression being denied but also the truth about the situation. Hence, the throat center is concerned with issues around justice/fairness and injustice/unfairness.

When in a state of balance, the throat center vibrates to the color sky-blue. This is often the color of healing energies as perceived by subtle sensing. If you find yourself suffering from a throat discomfort, like those described above, it can be relieved by visualizing that you are breathing a sky-blue-colored light into the throat. Do this slowly and gently with six breaths, letting go of the pain and thoughts and feelings about the issue with the out-breath.

The Brow Center

Located in the middle of the forehead, just above the brow, the brow center links with the body via the pituitary gland and hypothalamus in the brain. It is concerned with the brain, eyes, and face. One of the roles of the brow center is to oversee the operation of the centers below it. When subtle energies arrive here for transmission to the crown, the brow will send them back down the system if they have not been processed (i.e., if we have not dealt with the relevant issues).

I described earlier how the physical body is based on the etheric template. A good illustration of this is the way the pituitary gland and hypothalamus mirror the activity of the brow center by controlling and monitoring the secretions of all the other endocrine glands.

The brow center processes information from our psychic awareness, or subtle sensing— our so-called sixth sense—as well as information from our intuitive awareness, or soul sensing. Both forms of energetic information are passed to the solar plexus center via the special energetic link between this center and the brow. In the solar plexus center, of course, energetic information meets with mind, which then attempts to understand it.

Psychic awareness enables us to be aware of subtle energetic phenomena, such as the light of the energy field around someone. It is the awareness that tells us, when we enter a room for example, that people have just had an argument. We actually pick up the vibrations of this happening before we even see their faces. The fabric of a building, for example, absorbs energy so that psychic awareness enables a sensitive person to become aware of past events that may have happened in that building. These energies are external to us.

Intuitive awareness, on the other hand, enables us to be aware of messages from the Higher Self and of information from the spiritual levels—energies that are internal.

Our problem with all of the input to and from the brow center is that once it is conveyed to the brain for interpretation, the mind steps in to act as uninvited consultant. But the mind is only able to compare received information with what it already knows and understands. If mind cannot match the information with our perceived life experience, it tends to put that information straight in the reject tray.

Consciously or unconsciously, we have all had plenty of fun and games with our brow center. Since ancient times, it has been represented as, and called, the Third Eye because a way of seeing beyond the ordinary or of seeing beyond the appearance of things seems to originate here. This is exactly what the brow can do in terms of both our psychic and intuitive awareness. Indeed, life is enhanced when we learn to use and trust these natural abilities. This is the brow center's challenge. For Distant Healers, the brow center is the intuitive link with our Higher Self during attunement, as well as with the Higher Self of the person we work with.

When balanced, the brow center vibrates to a deep royal blue or indigo light.

The Crown Center

Located at the crown of the head, this center is our link with the Source and provides a spiritual link with all other beings of Light. The crown center deals with all issues of our spirituality, and it challenges us to acknowledge the spiritual truth of being and to allow this truth to be fully expressed in our lives.

The crown center links with the body via the pineal gland, which tells us about the amount of sunlight we are getting and whether we are getting enough. This gland also mirrors the crown center's role of telling us about the amount of spiritual Light we are allowing into our life and whether this is enough. When we do not get enough sunlight, as those who live in gray climates well know, we feel depressed. If deprivation goes on long enough, this can become the medical condition known as seasonal affective disorder (SAD syndrome). The remedy is to get some sunlight as soon as possible.

Deep depression or despair is very often a symptom of spiritual lack. This is why many cultures see such states as a disease of the spirit, a disease that should be tackled immediately. The remedy, of course, is a good dose of spiritual Light, which may not be the same thing as religion.

The special energetic link with the base center tells us that life is not about being either spiritual or human, but both. Life is a spiritual event, and we, and all other beings, are an expression of the Divine. The indigenous Lakota (or Sioux) people of North America proclaim this idea during any sacred act or ceremony when they pray, *"Mitákuye oyásin!"* ("We are all related!") When we are living this expression of Oneness, the crown center vibrates to the color violet.

The Human Rainbow

At a subtle level, we are walking rainbows. All the primary colors are needed to make a rainbow, and the fact that our energy centers vibrate to the colors of the rainbow tells us that our life is, and always was, a complete whole. There is no issue or experience that does not have a valid place in our unique story. With this in mind, it is helpful to recall the functions of the seven main centers in relation to our total being. The lower three centers, via the mind, exert a pressure on the personality to engage in humanness.

The personality may well, and often does, interpret its view of human life as all there is. The mind then tells us that there is plenty of logical and scientific argument to support this view. The upper three centers of the crown, brow, and throat, via our intuition and feelings, exert a pressure on the personality to recall our light, or spiritual, origins.

The heart center shows us that we will only be half of what we can be until we make the leap of faith and trust in our reality as soul. Through its processing of love issues, the heart center shows us that love is the key to a harmonious balance of both aspects of our being. This is the message of all seven levels of consciousness, especially the crown and heart.

The Centers of the Hands and Feet

Two further sets of subtle energy centers help us keep our links with planet Earth, with the "heavens," and with the expression of love that joins these two sacred aspects of being. The soles of the feet and the palm centers link the polarity of the planetary energies with the two etheric polarity channels. In healing, these channels are accessed via the soles of the feet and the tops of the arms.

Linked energetically with the base center, the centers in the soles of the feet absorb energies from the Earth (see Figure 15, on page 90). These life-giving energies are essential to the physical body and physical life. This is why it is good to walk barefoot outside whenever you can, a practice that will lead to the pleasure of sensing the Earth in a deeper way. The soles of the feet act as grounding or earthing points, as does the base center, for incoming subtle energies.

In the subtle sciences of Qi Gong and acupuncture, the *yongquan* point on the sole of the foot is connected to the kidneys and is a focus for treatment in cases of hypertension. This acupuncture point is in the same place as the sole of the foot center (just behind the center of the two large pads at the front of the foot). Its function gives a clue to the link between the centers of the feet and the base, because the base center energies enter the body via the adrenal glands. Let's see what you can sense with your foot centers.

exercise 26 **SENSING EARTH ENERGIES WITH THE SOLE-OF-THE-FOOT CENTERS**

• Stand on the ground in a relaxed posture with bare feet a shoulder-width apart. Take six slow breaths into the abdomen to attune yourself. Breathe normally.

• Put your mind in the soles of your feet. Be aware of your contact with the Earth, as well as with the grass, soil, sand, or whatever is under your feet. Close your eyes and notice whether you can sense an energetic transaction via the soles of your feet.

• Still with your focus in the feet, use the in-breath to aid your awareness of the passage of energy from the ground into your feet, up your legs, to the base center. Inhale a few times with this intention.

• Note your discoveries. Repeat the exercise in different locations and at different times of the day. What did you discover?

In Qi Gong, the *laogong* point on the palm of the hand is related to the heart, blood circulation, and the release of negative *qi*, or heavy energy. This clue tells us about the vital energetic link between the palm centers and the heart (Figure 15, page 90). The link means that the palms of each hand can act as extensions of the heart in conveying love and healing. Hence we soothe, touch, and caress with the hands. When the hands are used to hurt another, there is a negative effect on the heart center. Try the next exercise to see if you can sense the hand-heart link.

exercise 27 SENSING THE HAND-HEART ENERGY CIRCUIT

This exercise extends the sensitivity you discovered and activated in the exercises so far. The first part focuses on drawing in energy; the second, on giving it out.

- Sit in a chair in a relaxed position with your legs uncrossed. Hold your palms out, facing away from you, with your arms bent at the elbow. Relax your elbows, the back of the neck, and the shoulders. Close your eyes if this helps your concentration. Breathe normally.

- Focus your attention on the palm centers. As you inhale, imagine that you are drawing energy in through the palm centers. Breathe out gently through the palms. Note your sensations.

- Now visualize the energetic link between your palms and your heart center. Breathe in and sense energy moving up your arms, across your shoulders, to converge in the heart center in the middle of your chest.

- Lower your arms and relax for a few moments. Raise your arms again, with your hands held out in front of you as before. In this second part of the exercise, you are going to send energy from the heart center to the palms.

- Focus on the heart center and relax. Breathe into the heart center. As you exhale, visualize energy moving from the heart center, out to the shoulders, down the arms, to the center in each palm. What did you sense this time?

- Compare your experiences of absorbing and transmitting energy via the palm and heart centers.

Your experiences with the last two exercises should reinforce your understanding of the role of the hands and feet in Distant Healing. The sole centers, through their contact with the planet, keep us grounded energetically and "earthing" energetic activity. Grounding ourselves is important for our efficient functioning as a channel for healing energies, especially in the advanced out-of-body work we will be coming to in Chapter 10. Through the palm centers, we transmit healing energies and absorb energetic information. During this activity, the centers act like a kind of subtle eye.

We have another way of keeping in touch with the "heavenly" realms, apart from the crown center. Although our hands may hang at our sides for much of the time, we can extend them in the opposite direction above our head. By holding the palm centers upward, we can visualize breathing in the energies of the sun, sky, and cosmos. This stance is a natural expression of joy and can be taken up to bring in positive feelings and to combat depression.

An issue for most Distant Healers, which also features on the agenda of most Distant Healing groups, is how to confront the feelings that surface during the work. These feelings can arise when the request for help is made, when compiling the working list, even during the session itself. We also need to add to this the effects of information and other life events on us.

The Distant Healing method presented in the next chapter provides positive ways of addressing the subject and ways of acquiring the important skills to address personal feelings and negativity during healing sessions.

Chapter 9

Addressing the Effects of Personal Feelings and Negative Energies

Feelings and Attunement

In my workshops on Distant Healing, a recurring subject is whether it is appropriate for us, as healers, to have feelings about our work. This question is inevitably countered with the assertion that the attunement process should be enough to keep us totally focused; personal feelings shouldn't come into it. My response is that both aspects of the work are true for most people. The attunement exercise in Chapter 1 (page 17) is designed to align us with the Source of healing energies, but the link between attunement and feelings is highly relevant for us. So I am going to describe the process I use in my workshops for addressing this subject by combining different responses from a number of typical workshop situations.

Whenever you practice any exercise, it is within the context of what is happening around you and within you. The process of attunement challenges you to be aware of your inner state, because remaining in your heart center depends on it. In honoring the attunement process, questions arise such as, What emotional energies are you bringing with you? Are you calm and untroubled? Are you so unsettled by news or information recently received that conscious breathing and relaxation can only partially balance your emotional state?

Perhaps you are quite serene and looking forward to the work until you come to read your list. Then, without warning, a particular case creates a feeling that catches you off guard. Or, having become comfortably settled within your regular group meeting, you are upset when another member suddenly bursts into tears. Are you still focused, or has your attention moved to the solar plexus center? In other words, where are you?

This brings us to the first and recurring problem: Is it all right to have feelings? On the positive side, we probably wouldn't want to do Distant Healing if we didn't care about others and the state of the world around us. This heartfelt feeling fuels positive motivation, energizing us to act. On the negative side, the world is bombarding us with information, from far away and closer to home. Because we are sensitive, caring people, we are affected by this information, especially when it is some kind of disturbing or intimidating news.

Group Experiences

At one workshop, the group was asked how they would respond to a common anxiety: Should I go to the meeting this evening when I'm feeling so churned up? Won't that affect the work of the group? If I tell them why I'm churned up, won't everyone be affected? Questions like these help the whole group. They press emotional buttons; in this case, some members even felt threatened. They preferred to feel in control and unaffected rather than admit the possibility that a news happening, injury to a loved one, or a death in the family could upset their equilibrium. Spirituality was about equanimity and control of the emotions.

We could have continued to discuss this, swinging back and forth between differing points of view. Instead, I asked the group to listen to a two-minute tape of some real, though harrowing, radio news items. Every item had happened somewhere in the world within the past week. After a short pause, I asked if anyone would like to share how they were feeling after hearing the tape.

A young woman of nineteen hung her head and sighed. "I'm afraid of the world. . . . because there's nothing I can do about it. Some days, I'm even afraid of being alive." The man sitting next to her nodded. He understood, because he was aware that he had had no education on how to deal with any form of negativity. He was filled with feelings that ranged from despair that he could do nothing to anger at his own helplessness.

There was some nervous moving about in seats, but by owning her feelings, the youngest member of the group had given everyone else permission to do the same. As others spoke up, it was soon obvious that the group felt an overwhelming sense of negativity and powerlessness. For some, this brought feelings of anger and despair. Others needed to tune out and simply ignore what they were hearing: "This is what you hear every day. You have to find a way to cope with it, or you'll be suicidal." "Turn it off—I turn it off! You don't have to listen to it."

I switched the focus to how they felt in their bodies. Some said they sensed uncomfortable feelings in the solar plexus center—sensations of pulling, churning, pain, burning, and "an attempt to close down" feeling. Sensations in the heart center were just as unpleasant—pulling, shrinking, squeezing, compression as if by a heavy weight, fogginess, loss of clarity, and a closing down of love.

Finding a Constructive Strategy

When we are honest with ourselves, we can at least admit that our emotional reactions to the media and other information affect our ability to work wholeheartedly as Distant Healers. It becomes obvious that we need a strategy that is more constructive than mere coping. I asked the group to engage with finding a solution that evolved from this awareness. Most of us had stopped reading newspapers, and some refused to listen to the news either on radio or on TV. But when we considered going on a "news strike," the group reluctantly agreed that, as healers, we should not cut ourselves off from what was happening around us or from happenings in the rest of the world. How could we send healing help if we weren't aware of all that was going on? The other position, however, was that these were good reasons for sticking to the "list" and working solely with requests for help. But again, the majority felt that this was a kind of shortsightedness at best, or an ostrich-like response at worst. Our times demanded that we look further than the list. We knew that positive thought can affect situations—how much more good could be done with Distant Healing. This brought us back to the need for a strategy that kept us in touch with news events, while encouraging us to work with them.

How the "List" Affects Us

At this point, I suggested that we should first look at whether simply stick-ing to the list really did shield us from feelings. To test this, we listened carefully as each of us read out our lists. Then I asked group members to describe their feelings on reading their own list and on hearing the lists of the rest of the group. First there came the urge and desire to help, a well-ing up of love in the heart center. There was a pause as we contemplated these fine feelings. Then, one by one, members owned up to feelings of guilt, anger, resentment, tiredness, and grief. Some confessed to letting their minds wander and realized this was a tuning-out strategy.

Initially, the group members were shocked by their own revelations. Distant Healing was an act of unconditional love. Why hadn't attunement kept them in the place of compassion? They looked around the circle at one another. There were long faces, sad faces, and bewildered faces.

Then suddenly there was a burst of laughter. "Look at us. We're so disap-pointed that we're not saints!" This remark broke the tension, and there was more laughter.

"I admit it," said a would-be saint. "Sometimes I'm really affected just hearing myself reading out my list. Then tonight it happened again while hearing other people's lists—realizing that each one of them was in trou-ble or was trying to deal with some problem." This brought tears to quite a few eyes.

The learning from all this is that we are deeply affected by the daily doses of negativity that come our way and also by the unending healing challenge they represent. A similar emotional challenge is presented by our encountering requests for help and then dealing with these requests. These emotional impacts affect us whether we choose to work solo or with a group.

The Two Energetic Situations

Two energetic situations emerged from our findings. In the first situation, the emotions that we generate within ourselves, for whatever reason, affect our energy centers, the endocrine glands, and the physical body. Their impact will be positive or negative, as I explain below. Second, information coming from outside us carries an actual energy. Energies like this also impact the centers and the physical body. In this second scenario, I will only describe what happens when the energy of *negative* news and information affects us.

Both of these energetic processes begin in the solar plexus center; they may happen separately or in tandem. Toward the end of this chapter, there are three exercises that, in combination, help us deal positively with these processes. This positive coping strategy will help you address energetic impacts, as well as your feelings and reactions.

Situation 1: How Our Emotions Affect the Centers and Glands

Emotions are first processed in the solar plexus center, which is linked to the mind and its messages. Any message received by this center activates the brow center. Recall that one of the tasks of this center is to pass intuitive, or soul, knowledge to us so that we can compare this with the mind's conditioned information. However, most people have a problem with accepting their intuitive wisdom, which goes on to affect different endocrine glands, producing a range of possible physical conditions.

If the solar plexus center receives a positive (life-enhancing, compatible, or loving) message, the brow center signals this to its "light" link with the pineal gland. This then triggers the thymus gland to strengthen the immune system, which, in turn, has a very positive effect on the heart center. These energetic activities explain how emotions influence the body, but they also explain how positive thinking and positive attitudes bring harmony, peace, and health to the system.

What happens, then, if the reverse takes place? If the solar plexus center receives a negative (life-denying, incompatible, or loveless) message, the brow center closes, preventing energetic flow in order to protect the route to the pineal and the gland itself. The pineal gland is not just sensitive to the amount of light in our physical environment; it is also sensitive to the amount of spiritual Light in our energetic environment. The effect of brow center closure on the pineal gland is to create pressure for more light.

This pressure only reinforces the closing of the brow. The unbalanced state of the pineal gland adversely affects the thymus gland, so that the immune system is also under threat and does not function efficiently. These energetic activities explain how trauma, negative emotional experiences, and negative attitudes influence the body and undermine its ability to fight off disease.

You are beginning to build up a picture of health outcomes that are the result of your emotional life. This adds to your essential knowledge base; you can apply this knowledge to yourself so that you remain healthy and able to do your healing work. Before you can do this, however, you have to understand that everything in life is radiating energy and that you need to be particularly aware of those energies that are moving toward you. This includes the negative energies of news and information.

Situation 2: How Negative-Information Energy Affects the Centers

The energetic impact of negative news, signals, and information creates a second, often parallel, response, which is just as damaging as that caused by our emotional reactions. In this case, we are looking at the impact of massive doses of negative energy on all the energy centers. These reactions will be taking place irrespective of our emotional response.

Our leaders, and others in positions of responsibility, probably do not realize what is happening to their citizens. If they did, they would have no idea how to deal with the problems. We must find our own way to deal with the impact on our personal world and with the effects on our energy centers.

The mind is the first part of us to absorb the negative energy of a message, whether from the media, a letter, a telephone message, or a conversation. We feel the impact as a threat to our sense of safety and security. This is because of the process outlined as follows: The mind cues the solar plexus center to receive the outside energies. The negative quality of these outside energies is interpreted as a threat, which triggers the defensive emotion of fear. This, in turn, generates the energies of stress and anxiety. These stresses impact the person's sense of self, as well as his or her sense of personal power and self-worth. At the same time, the digestive system and nearby organs are affected via the endocrine glands in the pancreas.

Ultimately, negative energies threaten personal survival so that the negative energy is pulled down toward the base center via the sacral

HALF PRICE BOOKS
2041 Ford Pkwy.
St. Paul, MN 55116
(651)6991391

05/21/14 03:00 PM
#00023/LHAR023/00001

CUSTOMER: 0000000000
SALE: 0001847728

1 @7.99   1004704820   7.99
10000000000100470482-Distant Healin

SHIP/HAND   0.00
TAX (7.625% on $7.99)   0.61
TOTAL   8.60

PAYMENT TYPE
CASH   20.00

PAYMENT TOTAL $ 20.00
CHANGE DUE - CASH $ 11.40

THANK YOU!

2041 Ford Parkway-St. Paul, MN
(651) 699-1391

Return policy on back of receipt

END OF TRANSACTION

the expression of joy, cre-
lower back are affected via

se center, where they, again,
ouraging detachment from
of aging, even fear of death.
via the adrenal glands, they
body.
heart centers, the energetic
center. The organs of the
evelop a sense that there is
rld.
throat center. The ear, nose,
The subtle effect is that we
ve cannot be who we really
t how we appear to others.
e devalued.
sical impact, via the pitu-
head, eyes, and brain. But
and their production of
ined, we lose trust in our
connection with knowing
l, we feel the need to put
s of others. We tend to
ices and instead look to a
e, to solve our problems.
hing is solved outside of
ening to and heeding our

ive energetic messages. A
oin with the mental and
emotional turmoil that incessant doses of negativity create. This center
processes all issues about our link with the Source and the Light of the
Source. We wonder if we can ever make contact with the Source within,
even if it did in fact exist.

The World Has an Impact on Every Energy Center

In this way, the world has an impact on every center and, through each center, on the physical body. The first signs that we, or our bodies, are trying to cope with high doses of negativity are the appearance of any of the symptoms described in the previous sections: stress, anxiety, tiredness, and the early stages of bodily disease.

But we should always remember that the body is our friend. It is designed and formed for life, even when some life events may be destructive. We are genetically endowed with the ability to withstand a certain level of negative effects. We must remember that life is also the manifestation of the divine Source, our true reality.

Our friend, the body, has various ways of warning us when the limits of tolerance have been reached. First, we should listen and take heed and be aware that the mind will often try to override bodily messages. Second, when the body is calling to us, problems may already be manifesting on the mental and emotional levels. The way we deal with negative energies will determine whether they have the power to nullify the life-affirming, life-building, health-creating energies of our own being. One way to ensure our health and safety is through the threefold empowerment strategy of accepting our feelings.

Accepting the Message of Our Feelings

The heart center is the balancing and harmonizing point in our physical and subtle energetic bodies. At the same time, it is the center that processes all issues concerned with love. It is where we find our response to lovelessness. This is where we attune to the Source, where our mental intention is given its soul dimension, and where the energies of healing emanate.

This is why the impact of emotions is so important in our work. Feelings and emotions in themselves are not good or bad, right or wrong. They carry no judgment or moral overtone. We should, however, listen to our feelings, because they are the language that the Higher Self uses to indicate whether something is appropriate for us. Our level of discomfort acts as a scale we can use to help us decide this.

A common feeling of discomfort occurs when feelings are not expressed. A lump in the throat—or pain, burning, or a feeling of blockage there—signals that some feeling is not being expressed and should be. When things in our life are not true or are not being expressed when they need to be, the throat center responds. This discomfort can also be the result of our not being creative or not doing what we feel we want to do in life. Sometimes these feelings result from our blocking our positive expressions of love and joy. We may even find that our own inhibitions urge us to block others' positive expressions.

Missing the Real Message

Returning to the Distant Healing Circle, we can see that it is possible to misinterpret the impact of positive energies—on us or on someone else—especially when the mind interprets those energies according to its own conditioning.

Once I was working with a group when a woman collapsed sobbing. Members who had never encountered this wondered if something had gone wrong. They wondered, too, why I did not jump up and pass her the box of tissues. This woman was later able to explain to the group how the influx of healing energy, with its powerful feelings of love and beauty, completely overwhelmed her. She was crying with joy!

This can happen to an individual whether working solo or in a group. It is not an emotion but a reaction to the energy of love. At such times, blocking the person's reactions by offering reassurance such as tissues or a pat on the back is not a loving gesture. The best reassurance is the silent, loving support of sitting with them, being there for them. People must be allowed to express what is happening within. It was an important experience for the group to learn to accept what can happen.

Body Awareness and Energetic Flow

Feelings, then, need to be welcomed, because they are expressions of energetic happenings and that energy needs to flow. Energetic flow allows the system to rebalance itself and return to harmony. An interruption to this process, no matter how well meant, creates an energy block. This is the key to the next three exercises, which are designed to help you address your feelings by permitting their energetic flow. We begin by becoming more deeply aware of our body.

exercise 28 **BODY AWARENESS**

- Sit or lie comfortably. Use your breath to relax your body. Allow your breathing to settle to a gentle rhythm.

- As you link with the rhythm of your breath, visualize that your body is surrounded by a sphere of golden light. Notice how you become calm and serene as your awareness of the normally peaceful operations within your body increases.

- Take a moment to remind yourself that this is the vehicle for your soul's expression on Earth. Your consciousness helped to make your body what it is today. You dwell within this body, where a million movements of energy are continually taking place. You can join the smallest or the greatest part of this activity through your link with the body consciousness.

- Gently scan your body. Notice where your attention is drawn first. Try to maintain this relaxed attention as you continue to scan your body.

- You are sitting or lying on something. Notice what this feels like. Notice what you sense, what you hear.

- Become aware of your breathing again and notice any feelings of discomfort. Without trying to interpret them, pay attention to these bodily sensations.

- As you relax into the light that surrounds you, allow yourself to be. Mentally affirm, "I am."

This body awareness exercise can be continued for as long as you wish, but it should be for not less than five minutes. As a simple tool for being with your body, it is another building block of Distant Healing.

exercise 29 **ACCESSING BODY SECRETS**

- In the same position as in Exercise 28, relax and breathe normally. Recall that the operations of the body are based in the cells. Because of energetic and cellular consciousness, the body is able to store memories about anything that has happened to it, from the time of conception until now.

- Allow your attention to focus on the first body part that comes to mind (don't think about it). Allow this part to show you what it has stored. Accept what comes without judgment. It may be in the form of pictures, words, or sensations.

If you have been ill or have suffered an injury, listen to what your body may have to tell you about it. If you locate a certain mood or feeling somewhere in your body, allow these parts of yourself to talk to you about your perceptions and sensations. By allowing your body to draw your attention to a certain part, your intuition comes into play. This part is speaking to you because it is the right moment to communicate what it has to say and for you to pay attention to this.

When communication has finished, see the golden glow of energy around you change to pink, the color of love, in your mind's eye. Allow this pink light to penetrate every part of your body. Give thanks for this light and its effects.

Working with Your Feelings: From Coping to Empowerment

In the two previous exercises, you had the opportunity to become aware of how feelings find a place in the body. Having become accustomed to how your body communicates this, you can further develop the relationship by addressing the issue we have been looking at—how to own our powerful feelings and how negative energies impact our systems—in a positive, constructive way. The next exercise completes the empowerment strategy.

In the first stage of the next exercise, we acknowledge that feelings and reactions arise in us. They originate in the subtle energy system; they are not simply created in the mind as fearful imaginings. Next, we recognize that they are energies and that this kind of energy should be kept moving, allowed to flow. In the second stage, we must accept our feelings and accept energetic impacts. This allows energetic flow. Once we can allow and encourage the flow of our own, as well as incoming energies, we will find that our systems can return us to a state of balance. Resistance works against this innate ability. Since we were children, we have learned to block energy flow. As Distant Healers, we now have to learn how to remove these blocks.

---

exercise 30 **WORKING WITH YOUR FEELINGS**

- Make sure that you will not be disturbed during this exercise. Sit or lie comfortably alone. It is not necessary to relax the body or do anything that will calm your feelings.

- Begin by focusing on how you are feeling. Don't worry about your breathing or relaxation. Notice your thoughts and what is going on in your body as you pay attention to your feelings.

- Increase your awareness of your feelings by deciding why you feel happy, why you feel uncomfortable, why you feel frightened, why you feel sad, and so on.

- Notice whether you tend to judge yourself. Notice whether you offer resistance to the exercise. Try to just observe and no more.

- Now deepen your experience of your feelings by simply accepting them unconditionally, just as they are right now. Relax into this acceptance. These are your feelings.

exercise continues >

- As you become aware of your breathing, breathe with the feelings as if you are aligning with them and flowing with them. Breathe your feelings.

- Now, as you gently take time, your breath and your feelings gradually come to a place of balance. Take your time. Stay with what you are now feeling.

- Bring your attention to your heart center, consciously opening it, as if you were opening the "arms of your heart." Welcome the balance of feelings into your heart center.

- Become aware of your whole being in a state of peace. Stay in this peace-filled awareness.

By becoming aware of your feelings, by identifying them, by accepting and experiencing them, you allow them to impact you, and you allow your reactions to them, so that you can be released into healing. By practicing this exercise, you will come to understand what feelings and emotions are. You are not your emotions. You realize that your emotions need not control you.

With the previous exercise, you *consciously* moved the fearful energies of the solar plexus center up into your heart center (instead of the unconscious movement of moving them down into the sacral center, as described earlier). You are consciously moving the energy flow to the place of balance and unconditional love. If you practice this exercise with a partner or a group, you will gain great benefits through sharing your experiences. The group energy also enhances the constructive process of the exercise.

In the case of your strong reaction to the flow of healing energies through you, through the group, or from one to another in your group, carry out the same procedure. Notice whether you are still in your heart center or whether your reactions, or the reactions of others, have moved the flow down to your solar plexus center.

Feelings are an important part of your energetic makeup. They are a reminder of who you are—essentially, a being of love. We all need to express love and receive love. Positive feelings are a natural expression of love. Negative feelings are a natural response to lovelessness. The personal challenge is not to add to the energies of lovelessness by word, thought, or deed— thereby closing down the system against love—but to return to the heart center. This is the challenge to Distant Healers with every call for help that they receive.

Having begun to study the energetic impact of living in the world, of absorbing negative energies, of confronting healing issues, or even of the effect of Love itself, you are better equipped to add some more advanced techniques to your way of working. Some of these may take you out of your physical body, which may sound strange but is actually quite natural. You move "out of your body" every night when you go to sleep, something you have been doing since you were in the womb!

Chapter 10

Advanced Distant Healing

Multidimensional You

If we become enclosed in our own feelings, we soon feel separation from others and the world, even separation from the wonder of the multidimensional self described in Chapter 3. I emphasize that we can avoid this by returning to the heart center, for here we are aligned with the source of multidimensional life. Here, we know that Distant Healing is possible because we are all one, united both energetically and spiritually. Here, we know that energy follows thought, because this is one of the laws of Love. Prayerful intention is a means of crossing all dimensions, instantly traveling to the source of creation, because the Source is actually within each of us, closer than breathing.

You know that you have a physical reality, an emotional reality, and a mental reality. Distant Healing is now going to introduce you to another aspect of your total spiritual reality. We are conscious of our body, our thoughts and feelings, and, from time to time, our dreams, plus all the sensory information that we take in from the world around us. But the possibility of being conscious of other levels is always there. In addition to sending out our healing intentions from our solo or group base, it is possible for us to make another kind of contact with the subjects that are at a distance from us. We may or may not be aware of this contact with our everyday consciousness. This usually depends on two factors: how necessary conscious contact is and our mental, intuitive, and spiritual development.

Life Outside of the Physical Body

At the end of Chapter 9, I mentioned how you have out-of-body experiences on a regular basis when you sleep. This is possible because the spiritual you, the Higher Self, is the real you. You were a reality before your body came into existence, and you will exist after your body ceases to be. You can, and do, detach yourself from the physical, with its etheric bridging level, to travel outside the space-time continuum. This enables you to do a range of things that you cannot do when confined to your physical body.

You can, for example, meet up with those who teach you; you can make contact with those who have passed over (so that everyone actually gets proof, during his or her own lifetime, that consciousness continues after physical death). Your mind then tries to make sense of this information and, more often than not, presents it to you as a dream.

When these dream experiences are not simply a means of sorting out what has been going on in your mind (such as the happenings of that day), they are probably out-of-body experiences. When your dream experience is vivid, unforgettable, and in color, it is a message from your Higher Self. You need to take time to absorb such messages. Your intuition, not your mind, will guide you. This is because the mind will only be able to compare it with previous data already stored. A better use of mind is to record such activities in order to enhance everyday living and your life journey.

The other important thing that happens is that you use the sleep state to travel out of your body to help and heal those in need. Again, your mind tries to make sense of that dream, too. The whole realm of healing in the sleep state is fascinating—not because you are able to do it, but because you are not conscious of it. In other words, the information is not transferred to your everyday awareness. Nevertheless, this is another aspect of Distant Healing.

I frequently receive telephone calls, letters, and e-mails from people all over the world, thanking me for appearing to somebody to help them. In most of these cases, I have no recollection of the encounter whatsoever, and they may not even be on my Distant Healing list!

These things are part of my experience, but you may feel the need for explanations. The pioneering work of physicists and mathematicians, such as Professor William A. Tiller, has done much to provide a scientific rationale for the phenomenon of out-of-body experiences. A very clear account of his work, as it applies to Distant Healing, appears in Dr. Richard Gerber's *Vibrational Medicine* (see references to both researchers in Further Reading, page 213, and Web Resources, page 217).

The Astral Level, Astral Traveling and Distant Healing

The phenomenon of traveling outside the physical body has always existed. In Western cultures, it came to be called *astral traveling*, derived from the Latin and ancient Greek for "star" (*astrum/astron*). We sleep when the stars appear; hence, "astral traveling" came to mean traveling in the sleep state, in your astral body, on the astral level. This so-called astral level is simply any level of being outside the physical, when you are in your astral body, which can happen at any time, not just when you are asleep. Being "out of body" is being in your astral body.

The astral body has a frequency band that, at its lowest range, lies between the etheric and the emotional energy zones.

Like the physical body, the astral body has energetic links to the etheric, emotional, mental, and soul energy zones. The subtle energy system pervades all these zones, and the energetic activity within them is conveyed to and from them via the energy centers.

Some healers are able to move on to the astral level to carry out Distant Healing during their waking state. This may be a conscious or unconscious experience. Thus, it is possible that some people may describe how the healer appeared to them, even when the healer has no waking knowledge of this.

In Distant Healing, energetic tracks or pathways are opened up so that conscious astral-level healing can occur in two basic ways. You find either that you can "travel" (in your astral body) to the person needing help or that the person is "brought" to you in their astral body. Some Distant Healers like to work this way, especially when there is an emergency call for their

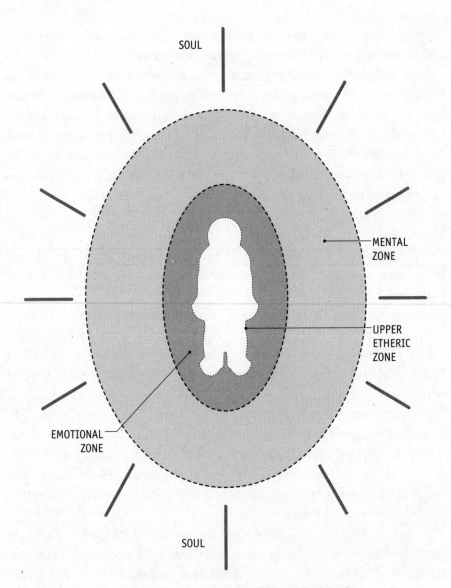

figure 19 **The Energy Field of the Astral Body**

help. It is quite possible to train yourself to travel in your astral body, but most healers have not reached this state of conscious control over their astral movements and are happy to rely on soul guidance about when and how the traveling will take place. I advise that you assume this attitude and go with the flow of soul, too.

In Distant Healing, keep it simple and natural at all times. The astral-level exercises, like all the exercises here, should only be used for the healing purposes specified.

Astral-Level Healing

The next exercise is designed to help you begin conscious astral-level healing, if you are guided, or inspired, to work this way. Although I describe it as an advanced way of working, it is a natural development of Distant Healing and of your own development as a Distant Healer. Practice it a number of times and keep a record of what you experience. This will enable you to assess which way you tend to work and what feels most comfortable for you.

If you have any queries about the exercise, get your working partner to join you as a passive observer and supporter. In the Introduction, I described how, when I got back from Italy, I soon found myself doing astral-level healing without even trying; it was the most natural way for me to work.

---

exercise 31 **ASTRAL-LEVEL HEALING**

Though you always work with the subject, rather than the condition, in astral-level work, you will often be aware of your hands moving into the area of a stated condition, as well as other important sites, such as the centers. Go with the flow of your guidance and make a note of what happens later.

- Make sure that you will not be interrupted in any way. Prepare and dedicate your working space. Have your list of subjects. Attune yourself, light your candle, and dedicate the work. Ask to be used as a channel for healing and to be guided by your Higher Self (soul). You will look forward to being directed by this source (whether or not you will be doing any Distant Healing at the astral level).

exercise continues >

- Sit with your feet flat on the floor with your hands palms up on your thighs or in your lap. Your hands should not overlap or touch. (In astral work, it is essential for the palm centers to remain active, hence the palms-up position of the hands.) Use your breath to calm and relax the body. Let go of any worries or anxieties with the out-breath through the open mouth.

- When you feel attuned, close your mouth and breathe normally. Check that your body is relaxed, including the back of the neck, the shoulders, and pelvis. Sit in silence for a few moments.

- Now take the first request on your list. Mention the subject by name, because the vibration of the name strengthens your link with the person (as in the Healing Triangle; see Figure 1, page 13).

- Close your eyes to aid with concentration. Wait quietly and patiently to see if you become aware that the subject is in front of you.

- If you have been "taken" to the person or the person has been "brought" to you, you will sense his or her presence. This becomes easier when you relax and accept that it is possible for this to happen. You will also be able to sense whether the adult person, child, or baby is lying or sitting in front of you and how the body is orientated.

- Mentally make sure that you are comfortably orientated to carry out what needs to be done. Allow your intuitive guidance to help you sense where your hands need to go.

- Let's take an example as an illustration: Your help has been requested for a man who has problems with movement on the

exercise continues >

right side of his body. In this case, once you are aware of his astral body in front of you, you will probably feel drawn to hold your hands over the area in question—the right side of his body. If this is what he needs, you will feel healing energy leave your hands, or whatever sign tells you that you are working. Move down the rest of the right side as far as you find energy to be needed.

- Keep your hands over each area until you feel a change in the flow of energy, which could be sensed as a marked decrease, or falling off, in intensity. This signals that all, or part, of the healing is complete.

figure 20 **Astral-Level Healing**

- Wait for your intuition's guidance to see if you need to give healing elsewhere. There may be a center involved, for example, or you may need to move your hands to somewhere else.

exercise continues >

- The energetic activity in your hands is confirmation that this is not taking place in your imagination. A person with developed perceptions would be able to sense or "see" what is going on and confirm that you are working this way.

- When you have completed your work, mentally thank the person you were working with. Now take a full breath and, as you exhale, surround him or her with a protective sphere of light. This may be done mentally or by raising your arms and moving your hands gently to make a sphere around the astral body in front of you.

figure 21 **Astral-Level Healing—The Sphere of Protection**

- At this point, either the Distant Healing subject returns to his or her physical body or you return to your physical body. You may also remain in the astral-body state to receive the next subject

exercise continues >

on your list in the same way. Or you may both return to the physical state.

- If there is another subject to work with, first make sure that the one you were working on is no longer in front of you (i.e., they have returned to their physical body). Visualize clear silver light washing over your upraised palms. You can now proceed to the next subject on your list. Take a short pause if you feel the need.

- Follow the same procedure as before. Break your link with the last subject by clearing your hands.

- When you have completed your work, blow out the candle. This can be done by sending out the light of the candle. Pause for a moment to see if you intuitively feel where the light needs to go. This is usually the first place that comes to mind. As you blow out the candle, say, "I send the Light out to . . . "

- Carry out the Closing-Down Procedure outlined in Chapter 5.

If during an astral-level healing you sense that you are no longer sitting in your chair, but are standing over or by the subject, you will know that you have traveled to him or her. Keep relaxed and proceed as described above. You are quite safe and can move out of this state whenever you like.

This way of working is very satisfying. Even so, it requires intense, but relaxed, concentration. Because of this, I recommend that you start astral-level healing with one subject at a time, with an aim of no more than six in any one session, unless guided otherwise. You need to feel totally comfortable and build up your confidence so that you do not get tired by the level of focused effort needed to work this way.

Keep a note of what happens in your healing journal and try to get some feedback about your work whenever possible.

Working Together

It is good to compare notes with another or others who are working on the astral level. Networking gives you the opportunity to share and gain knowledge and insight from the experience of others. It acts as a form of peer supervision and helps to keep everyone's "feet on the ground." This can be done with your Distant Healing Circle, as you all aim to work on the astral level. As before, you will need someone to lead or facilitate each time you meet, and every member should take a turn as facilitator. In the following exercises, I suggest two basic ways of working.

---

exercise 32 **THE ASTRAL-LEVEL HEALING CIRCLE—WITH ONE JOINT LIST**

Before working together, the whole of this exercise should be read to the group so that everyone is clear about how to proceed.

Make sure that you will not be disturbed; disconnect all telephones. Arrange the chairs in a circle in the center of which is a candle that can be placed safely on the ground. The group should have one list that you have compiled together. The length of the list will be dictated by the time you have together but should have no more than six to ten tasks on it, unless intuitively guided otherwise. The group agrees on one nominated member to carry out the work as outlined below.

- The group sits in a circle with feet flat on the floor and their hands palms up on their thighs or in their laps. The hands should not overlap or touch. The group leader should help the group to attune and follow these guidelines.

- "Use your breath to calm and relax your body. Let go of any worries or anxieties with your out-breath, through the open mouth. When you feel attuned, close your mouth and breathe normally. Check

exercise continues >

---

figure 22 **The Astral-Level Healing Circle**

that your body is relaxed, including the back of your neck, shoulders, and pelvis. Allow the calm silence to settle on our Circle."

- The leader lights the candle and dedicates the light to the work of the Distant Healing Circle, asking for the protection and guidance of the Source of healing energies.

- "Visualize the light of the candle as the light of these energies and breathe it in to the heart center. Allow the light to fill your chest."

- "Now, pass the energy in your heart center to the person on your left, until you are all linked together." Intuitively, you may have to wait to gather your heart energy before you can pass it on.

exercise continues >

- The leader should be aware of this and allow enough time for group linking, for this is the foundation of the Healing Circle. Most people will sense when the circle is linked.

- The leader expresses the purpose of the meeting and gives thanks, on behalf of the group, for the opportunity to be of service. "Focus on the Light in the heart center. See this Light extending from you to the center of the Circle. This builds a central column of Light—the Light of healing."

- The leader announces the group's first task: "We ask to be used as channels for healing for (the name of the person, animal, situation, and so on, on the list)."

- The group waits for the subject to appear (to their inner vision) in the center of the circle.

- As soon as a nominated member is chosen, he or she should begin work on the subject, just as in Exercise 31 (page 127). The rest of the group contributes to the healing by sitting in awareness, creating a powerful group energy that will be used in the healing work. At this stage, members may sense energy moving from their hands.

- Other group members may feel intuitively that they need to use their hands also. This should only occur once the nominated healer has begun to work.

- The leader monitors group activity. Work is completed on the first named subject when the healer has ceased hand activity and returned his or her hands to the resting position (palms down).

exercise continues >

The leader indicates this to the group with a gentle signal, such as with a bell or with the words, "We have completed the work for (name)." On hearing this, group members return their hands to the resting position.

- The leader then announces the next task, and the group proceeds as before, with a different nominated healer each time.

- When the list is complete, the leader indicates this to the group. The group then sits together in the silence.

- The leader closes the Circle by expressing thanks, on behalf of the group, and by sending the Light out to where it is needed. This is usually the first place that comes to mind.

- Every member of the group takes steps to become well grounded by rubbing their hands together and becoming aware of their feet in contact with the ground. The leader checks that everyone is grounded. The group can celebrate their heart-based work in whatever way seems appropriate.

- Discuss your work together. Share experiences and queries to consolidate learning. During this reflection session, allocate time to make notes or to illustrate the experience in some way. This allows members to log their experience and learning, chart the energies they have been working with, and ground the experience. It also gives the mind time to absorb what has happened and for it to log the naturalness of this form of altered-state work.

The Circle could be followed by a group activity such as meditating, giving a reading, listening to music, and so forth. In the case

exercise continues >

of meditation, because it is a continuation of the same altered state of consciousness, it should take place before closing the Circle, as described above. Afterward, the leader sends out the Light and makes sure everyone is grounded. Before the group disperses, carry out the Closing-Down Procedure (Chapter 5) together.

The second basic astral-level healing method is very much like the procedure for working solo, but instead you are working with the support and energy of the group.

exercise 33 **THE ASTRAL-LEVEL HEALING CIRCLE— WITH INDIVIDUAL LISTS**

Before working together, the whole of this exercise should be read to the group so that everyone is clear about how to proceed.

Make sure that you will not be disturbed; disconnect all telephones. Arrange the chairs in a circle in the center of which is a candle that can be safely placed on the ground. Every member of the group should have his or her own list ready. The length of the list will be dictated by the time you have together but should contain no more than six to ten tasks, unless intuitively guided otherwise. The nominated group leader does not have a list, but instead monitors what is happening to every member and the Circle as a whole. Though you always work with the subject, rather than the condition, in astral-level work, you will often be aware of your hands moving into the area of a stated condition, as well as to other important sites, such as the centers. Go with the flow of your guidance and make a note of what happens later.

- The group sits in a circle with feet flat on the floor and their hands palms up on their thighs or in their laps. The hands should not

exercise continues >

overlap or touch. The leader helps the group to attune and follow these guidelines:

- "Use your breath to calm and relax your body. Let go of any worries or anxieties with your out-breath through the open mouth. When you feel attuned, close your mouth and breathe normally. Check that your body is relaxed, including the back of your neck, shoulders, and pelvis. Allow the calm silence to settle on our Circle."

- The leader lights the candle and dedicates the light to the work of the Distant Healing Circle, asking for the protection and guidance of the Source of healing energies.

- "Visualize the light of the candle as the Light of these energies and breathe it in to the heart center. Allow the Light to fill your chest.

- "Now, pass the energy in your heart center to the person on your left, until you are all linked together." Intuitively, you may have to wait to gather your heart energy before you can pass it on. The group leader should be aware of the group's need for a moment and allow enough time for group linking, for this is the foundation of the Healing Circle. Most people will sense when the Circle is linked.

- The leader expresses the purpose of the meeting and gives thanks, on behalf of the group, for the opportunity to be of service. "Focus on the Light in the heart center. See this Light extending from you to the center of the Circle. This builds a central column of Light—the Light of healing."

- The leader announces the group's task: "We ask to be used as channels for healing for those we each name mentally."

exercise continues >

- Each group member waits for their first subject to appear (to their inner vision) in front of them. As soon as they are aware of the person's presence, they begin work on the subject, just as in Exercise 31 (page 127), so that members are working simultaneously. Each member should take the time needed for the task. The whole group is also creating a powerful energy that will be used in each person's healing work.

- The leader monitors group activity, keeping an eye on the progress of the whole circle. In so doing, the leader also contributes to the group energy.

- Work is completed on the first named subject when you sense that hand activity has ceased. Return hands to the resting position (palms down).

- Take a few moments before choosing the next subject on your list. Work with him or her in the same way. When you have completed your list, return your hands to the resting position. Wait patiently for the leader to signal that everyone has completed their task list. Realize that you are still contributing to the group energy during this time.

- When every member of the group has reached the point of completion, the leader indicates this to the group with a gentle signal, such as a bell or the words, "We have completed our work. Let us sit together in the silence."

- The leader closes the Circle by expressing thanks, on behalf of the group, and by sending the Light out to where it is needed. This is usually the first place that comes to mind.

exercise continues >

- Every member takes steps to become well grounded by rubbing their hands together and becoming aware of their feet in contact with the ground. The leader checks that everyone is grounded. The group can celebrate their heart-based work in whatever way seems appropriate.

- Discuss your work together. Share experiences and queries to consolidate learning. During this reflection session, allocate time to make notes or to illustrate the experience in some way. This allows the group members to log their experience and learning, chart the energies they have been working with, and ground the experience. It also gives the mind time to absorb what has happened and to log the naturalness of this form of altered-state work.

The Circle could be followed by a group activity, such as meditating, giving a reading, listening to music, and so forth. In the case of meditation, because it is a continuation of the same altered state of consciousness, it should take place before closing the Circle, as described above. Afterward, the leader sends out the Light and makes sure everyone is grounded. Before the group disperses, carry out the Closing-Down Procedure (Chapter 5) together.

The two basic ways of astral-level healing could be alternated. Or members may have a preference and the group can decide on a common way of working together.

Distant Healing and Life Issues

Common requests for Distant Healing include help needed for the terminally ill, individuals who are about to pass over, and the bereaved loved ones they leave behind. Sometimes you might be asked to help an individual who has already passed over. Families also ask for help when a baby is expected; in that case, the healing will be directed to the mother, the incoming soul, and the obstetric and nursing team involved. Similarly, when a person is undergoing a serious operation or medical procedure, healing is directed to that person and to the medical team. This may also include other helpers and carers—cleaners and orderlies are a vital part of the healing picture, too.

All such situations greatly benefit from the healing energies summoned up and channeled through the different forms of group work outlined in this book. In this way, Distant Healing very often plays a part in the sacred occasions of birth, death, and therapeutic procedure.

Extending Your Experience

By practicing the exercises and carefully evaluating each one, you now have a range of practical ways to develop your experience and confidence. You are equipped to work alone or with a group. So far, we have concentrated on working with human subjects, although I have hinted that this could just be the beginning of what you want to do with Distant Healing.

The focus for us, all the way through, has been on the heart center, the center that processes all issues of love. But the heart center is first and foremost the place of the Higher Self and the place from which love emanates while you are working as a Distant Healer. I will be returning to the subject of the heart center in the final chapter to emphasize its preeminence.

I mentioned earlier that Distant Healing works because of Oneness. We are one with every human, every animal, every plant, the whole natural world, the planet and, yes, the rest of the cosmos. Love is Oneness in action. This means that we can extend our work into any of these areas. It also means that, as Distant Healers, we have to consider the activities of humans in relation to themselves and to the rest of the world.

From now on, we have to decide how we are going to respond to violence, crisis, and disaster—local, national, and global. Because this is one of the two fundamental issues for all healers in this new century, I give it special prominence by making it the issue of the penultimate chapter. Before that, however, let's return to another important and interesting way to extend the work by looking at the whole realm of how to send Distant Healing to animals, plants, and the environment.

part three

Chapter 11

Working with the Environment

We are all connected: each with each, all with all. Not mysticism: just biology.
Moral: as we seek to save the world, so we get closer to saving ourselves.

—**Simon Barnes**, "No Island Is an Island" in *Birds*

(the magazine of the Royal Society for the Protection of Birds), Winter 2006

The Environment Calls for Our Help

As we engage with life, we not only come into energetic contact with other human beings; we also make contact with the mineral, plant, and animal worlds. Most of the time, we are not aware of these contacts; our consciousness is otherwise engaged. But this is changing; more and more, people are recognizing our interrelationship with the natural world, how we affect it, and, now, more dramatically, how it can affect us. Today, the elemental group energies of earth, air, fire, and water, which shape our environment, are calling out for help.

All Life Is Conscious

We may be used to the presence of an ocean, a river, a lake, a mountain, a hill, a plain, a garden, and so on. Either they are part of our local landscape, or we spend periods of leisure with them. We also make contact with other elemental bodies, such as wind, clouds, and the warmth and light of the sun, rain, snow, and ice. But when elemental group energies impact us (through a stormy sea, a flooding river, a landslide, a hurricane, a forest fire, a volcanic eruption), we become much more conscious of them.

The wisdom of indigenous peoples, especially the shamanic, has always acknowledged these natural forms of consciousness, recognizing them as "beings" in their own right, whose collective consciousness is a force or power. This wisdom has come from direct experience of these energetic forms. But we do not have to belong to a shamanic or indigenous community to commune with natural consciousness. As the celebrated pioneer of interspecies communication, Dorothy Maclean, has shown, this consciousness is available to all those who are prepared to open their minds and hearts, thus enabling the intuitive brow center. This ability for us to connect more deeply with plants and animals has always been there, but we have denied the subtle sensitivity within us for so long that it has almost become extinct.

During her groundbreaking work as cofounder of the Findhorn Community in Scotland, Dorothy Maclean communicated with the overlighting spiritual forces of plants, the elements, and the landscape. These often take the form of group souls or spirits. From these sources, she received numerous beautiful and enlightening transmissions, which became, in effect, dialogues (see, for example, *To Honor the Earth* in Further Reading, page 213). The transmissions indicate that the whole of Nature sees human beings as part of the one web of life in which each part has a unique and vital role. They also demonstrate that because all aspects of Creation are conscious, we can communicate with them. This is a law of energy that has, throughout the ages, made possible the seemingly wondrous happenings created by healers, holy people, and shamanic practitioners.

We hear of the extinction of thousands of plant and animal beings, even of certain human groups. With extinction, the energy patterns and the wisdom of those beings are lost to us. The total effect on our group consciousness is extremely negative. The picture that we currently see is of unhealthy, unbalanced human beings attempting to live in an environment that they are progressively making unhealthy and unbalanced. To restore its state of balance, the environment is fighting back, as we are finding to our cost. At a soul level, we know what is happening, and the Higher Self is trying to get this awareness through to us. So we are living in a time when there is tremendous pressure from the soul level to wake up and become aware of the reality of what is happening and to stop living in virtual reality.

Distant Healing, through its understanding of conscious energy, has much to offer in facilitating the changes as species evolve, in preserving those patterns of consciousness that are in danger of disappearing, and in recovering the wisdom of those that have already disappeared. This is just one form of healing, through which we can offer a vital contribution to the goal of restoring planetary balance and harmony.

Distant Healing Is Communication with Consciousness

The beings that dwell here with us are spiritually and energetically our brothers and sisters. Their energy patterns can be seen by inner vision as patterns of light, like the human pattern of light I described in Chapter 3. Your energy pattern merges with the energy pattern of anyone or anything near you. They merge with the light of the ground you both stand on. Your light merges with the light of the air that you breathe and that surrounds you. Your light merges with the energy of the water you drink and with the energy of the food you eat. The whole flow of life is a vast movement of energy and an intricate pattern of light.

The Source, the Light, and consciousness are one, and we communicate with this consciousness. This is why Distant Healers dedicate their work to the Light, work as channels for the Light, put their subjects in the Light, or send Light to those beings and situations that need help. So when Distant Healers utilize the Light through this conscious intention, they are effectively proclaiming, "Let there be Light!"

Shedding Light on the Environmental Crisis

Many indigenous groups, such as the Native Americans and the Q'ero people of the Andes, have been speaking about the raising of human consciousness for some three or more decades. By this they mean that there is growing pressure from the spiritual levels for us to acknowledge the spiritual reality of all that is. A natural development of this raising of consciousness is the understanding and acceptance of Oneness.

This idea may seem new to many, especially to those brought up in certain religions, but the concept of Sacred Unity has always been a part of many traditions, and it has been the teaching of mystics the world over, not as an intellectual or philosophical notion but as an existential experience.

These traditions may smile at the irony of the "rediscovery" of Oneness (see, for example, any of the excellent *Conversations with God* series in Further Reading, page 213), but it is still an occasion for celebration. We can hope that this rediscovery has happened in time to begin the unification of human beings with one another and with the natural world.

In the past, the relationship between city-based cultures and Nature was greatly influenced by the doctrine of patriarchal religions and later by the mechanistic worldview of rational science. This relationship was based on the premise that human beings are obviously the dominant species, with a God-given or inherent right to dominate, subdue, and exploit the natural world for human benefit alone. For centuries, this premise was extended by the various colonial powers to indigenous humans, who had to be overcome, subdued, and exploited. The same attitude was perpetuated by the Industrial Revolution and its modern offspring of continuous production and technological development—at all costs.

In contrast, early sacred traditions held respect for Nature and its life forms. Human beings were part of an interdependent family of beings in which the natural world was to be cooperated with, not overcome. This cooperation was greatly facilitated by communicating with Nature. As the developed world now faces the global environmental crisis that has arisen through *noncooperation* with Nature, the raising of consciousness has led to an encouraging determination to engage with the issues.

A range of environmental organizations around the world are working hard to heighten awareness and suggest practical solutions. Universities, colleges, and schools are offering degrees and courses in environmental subjects. At the level of the individual, we can now recycle materials, take measures to avoid pollution, try to source our food locally as much as possible, become aware of how our own lifestyle affects the globe, and make appropriate choices for change. This "green," eco-friendly agenda implies a new respect for Nature and a movement toward honoring the indigenous wisdom that is still available to us all.

The Green Agenda for Distant Healing

In most parts of the world, when humans need to relax and de-stress, they gravitate toward the green of Nature. When the planet is in balance, plant life returns to its natural place, even when the natural place is a desert. It is no coincidence that the color of balance is green. When our subtle energy system is in balance, the heart center vibrates to the color green. The new agenda for Distant Healing is literally a green one in the sense that it mobilizes the soul force of the heart center to aid the worldwide effort to redress the imbalance that centuries of environmental abuse have brought about.

Again, shamanic cultures have had cause to smile over the scientific debate about whether planet Earth is a living being. In the 1960s, scientist James Lovelock proposed the ecological theory that the living matter of the planet functions like a single organism. This was virtually ignored in scientific circles until Lovelock popularized his theory in his books *The Quest for Gaia* (1975) and *Gaia: A New Look at Life on Earth* (1979). Lovelock named this self-regulating system after the Greek goddess Gaia (Earth). Then, after ten years of scientific criticism, Lovelock declared that there was no conscious purpose behind planetary self-regulation. Professor Lynn Margulis, who was principal collaborator with James Lovelock for twenty-five years, has stressed that Gaia is not an organism or a being (*The Symbiotic Planet: A New Look at Evolution*, 1998). However, new age, as well as environmental, circles have welcomed the personification of Gaia, seeing it as an assenting, if grudging, nod to indigenous concepts of Earth as mother and nurturer and certainly as a being.

Whatever the debate, transmissions from the natural world, such as those via Dorothy Maclean, indicate that both plant and environmental forces are doing their best to redress the imbalance caused by our activities, even sending healing to us. But they stress that a change to an eco-friendly lifestyle and sending out healing to the world are what is most needed. This coincides with the entreaties of shamanic populations worldwide to heed the voice of Nature and begin the process of healing without delay. This is also the green heart agenda of Distant Healing.

Communicating with the Elements

To work as a Distant Healer with the Earth and the Earth family, you first need to make sure that you can open your lines of communication with them. Our subtle energy system mirrors that of the planet, and our need for the right relationship with the Earth begins here. On the physical level, we are composed of all the four essential elements of life, just like the planet is. The body is linked to the element earth and the base center. The various fluids of the body (most of us are composed of around 75 percent water) are linked to the element water and the sacral center. The energy of the animating life force, and the heat of the body, is linked to the element fire and the solar plexus center. Our breath is linked to the element air, the life force, and the heart center.

It is well known that the ancient esoteric science of astrology also highlights our individual link with the four elements, so that each of us is an earth, water, fire, or air sign. (If you are not sure what your element is, look up your sun sign.) This comes about through our soul choice of when to be born, which gives each of us an affinity with the relevant element. When you come to working with the environment, make a note of the type of situations or subjects you feel drawn to. Ask yourself if they tend to be mainly earth-based, water-based, and so on.

Through our physical makeup of elements, we can see that what happens to the planet, energetically, is reflected in us, and what happens to us is mirrored in the state of the planet. This is what you will discover when you open your lines of communication to engage with your environment. Communication with the environment begins by acknowledging your relationship with the four elements that form the environment. Let's take this exciting opportunity to commune with the environments that surround us.

---

exercise 34 **COMMUNING WITH THE EARTH**

Before Native Americans enter the purification (sweat) lodge, they first give thanks to the Earth in the standing position. Then, in the kneeling position, they honor the Earth by touching the ground with their foreheads. This exercise makes use of that formula. If you are unable to take up the bodily positions described, the exercise may still be done through your mental intention and visualization.

exercise continues >

- Stand on the ground with your bare feet shoulder-width apart and your knees gently flexed. Use your breathing to relax, but remain totally aware. You are making subtle contact via the energy centers in the soles of your feet. Take six breaths as if you could breathe in the energy of the Earth through the soles of your feet. As you exhale, you share your energies with the Earth.

- Recall an enjoyable walk. Recall the feeling of working with the land. Remember when the sight of a certain landscape gave you joy. All beings come from this Earth and are nourished by it. When you engage with the Earth like this, you are offering your gratitude.

- Now assume a kneeling position as you honor the Earth. Take a full breath in this position.

- Touch the ground with your forehead (brow center). This makes contact between the Earth and your visionary self, your intuitive self. Breathe the Earth into your brow center.

- Now assume a sitting position so that the base of your spine is in contact with the ground. Breathe into the Earth via your base center.

- From the sitting position, lie down with your back touching the ground. Breathe in the energies of the Earth through the whole of your back. Exhale from your back into the ground.

- Stand up again and relax. When you engage with the Earth like this, you are acknowledging it and communing with it. See if you can engage in this wordless dialogue.

exercise continues >

- As you stand on the ground once again, you appreciate that all visions, all subtle sensations, are grounded in the physical body. This is where you are. The place where you stand is holy ground.

You will have picked up a range of sensations during this exercise. Perhaps Earth spoke to you. As you practice, the range of sensations will expand. Make a note of them in your Distant Healing journal. Practice in various locations and note any differences. Now engage with the other three elements.

exercise 35 **COMMUNING WITH WATER**
Find a natural source of water, large or small.

- Stand or sit near the water source you have chosen (or which has chosen you). Use your breathing to relax your body. Note everything that this particular source is conveying to you.

- Become aware of your breathing as you breathe into the sacral center. Breathe naturally. Water quenches your thirst, as well as the thirst of the land and plants. Recall a time when you simply enjoyed drinking fresh water. Remember listening to the soothing sound of rain outside. You are communing with the element of water.

- Allow water to "speak" to you. Feel that you can absorb what it is communicating via your sacral center. Close the exercise with your thanks.

- When you engage with water like this, you are acknowledging it and communing with it. See if you can engage in this dialogue, which may be without words.

exercise continues >

- Practice this exercise with a different source of water. Notice any differences between, say, an ocean and a lake, a river and a tiny stream. Remember that other sources like rain, snow, ice, and a waterfall can all be engaged with.

exercise 36 **COMMUNING WITH FIRE**

This exercise can be done in the same way with a fire outdoors or indoors, while you acknowledge the energy of fire as the release of the energy of the sun.

- Stand on the ground with your bare feet shoulder-width apart and your knees gently flexed. Use your breathing to relax, but remain totally aware. Face the direction of the sun (in the morning, this is in the east).

- Close your eyes. Become aware of your breathing as you breathe into your solar plexus center. Visualize that you are able to breathe the light of the sun into this center. You need the warmth and vitality of the sun. The skin of your body needs its rays to keep you healthy. Remember the feeling of waking up to a sunny day. Recall happy times in the sun. You are communing with the element of fire. Let your natural rhythm of breath be a thank you to fire.

- Allow fire to speak to you.

- As you engage with fire, allow any feelings to pass and move on, without comment or judgment.

- Change your body posture and/or location. Note any changes in your communion with fire.

exercise 37 **COMMUNING WITH AIR**
If possible, practice this exercise outdoors.

• Stand on the ground with your bare feet shoulder-width apart and your knees gently flexed. Use your breathing to relax, but remain totally aware.

• Become aware of your breathing as you breathe into your heart center. Air carries the animating life force and the oxygen that your body needs. It also carries the waste gases that your body discards. It carries the scent of the breeze, the flowers, the trees, and the sea. You are communing with the element of air. Let your natural rhythm of breath be a thank you to air. Allow air to speak to you.

• How does air move right now? What does this feel like?

• Change your body position and/or location. Note any changes in your communion with air.

From a Distant Healing point of view, the great need for environmental healing stems from the disruption of energetic flow and the millions of disconnections in the energy web that links the Earth with humans and with the rest of the Earth family. This is what you need to be aware of when you feel motivated to work with the environment. One of the single most devastating causes of the disruption of energy flow is our sense of separation from the natural world, which has resulted in the breakdown of relationship.

The list of disconnections between us and the natural world is long, and you could create your own. These disconnections allow us to do harmful things to the environment—such as gouge a way through the land for a new road—in such a way that the energy flow of the land and all the beings dwelling on it are interrupted. A simple ceremony of thanking and honoring the land where the road was made would have gone a long way to repairing the energy web. This is where Distant Healing has much to offer.

The exercises I have mentioned not only help you acknowledge your link with the four elements of the environment, they also help you reconnect with those elements. Now you need to look at how the elements compose the natural world around you. Become aware of the climate, the movement of air and water, the ground beneath your feet, the features of the landscape, and the signs of the seasons. Even if you live in the middle of a city, your home is rooted in Nature and depends on it. You breathe the air of the city, you drink the water, you eat the food that was grown somewhere. You need sources of warmth to stay alive. Now it is time to engage with your landscape.

exercise 38 **ENGAGING WITH YOUR LANDSCAPE**

- Go somewhere outdoors where you can sit comfortably. Take a few full breaths to help you relax your body. The goal of the exercise is to be fully relaxed, while at the same time being fully aware.

- Now attune to what is before you, beginning with the light. Become aware of what is nearby. What can you see?

- Close your eyes and listen. What do you hear?

- Pay attention to stillness, birdsong, rustlings, and movement; to the feel of the air and the feeling of the day; to the behavior of the clouds; and so on.

As you honor each part of the life around you, you expand your boundaries on all levels. This deepens your perception of, and alignment with, healing energies. Regular practice of this exercise will reveal many life secrets.

figure 23 **A Disrupted Landscape**

The Disrupted Landscape and Oceans

If you took a trip to a landscape that is special to you, you probably noticed places that had been disrupted in some way: a new road, a housing development, a factory project, and so on. All such operations involve energetic disruption. Furthermore, they usually involve a range of polluting factors. Aboriginal people would tell you that none of these things were done "in a sacred manner" by acknowledging our oneness with the land. Instead, the attitude was that the land is there to be used; it has no consciousness or feelings.

If you brought one of those sights to mind and held your hands up to see if healing was needed, your hands would probably signal that it was. Recall how I started Distant Healing with the Italian grandfather. My inner urge was to help, and my hands knew what to do. If the old man had not needed help, my hands would not have responded.

The next exercise deals with how you can respond to an environmental challenge, whether a local need or a global problem.

A new highway is being built near where I live. When this two-year project is completed, it is hoped that the traffic on this busy route will flow more quickly and freely. The work has meant digging out huge swaths of land that have to be dumped somewhere else. Trees have been cut down and natural habitats destroyed.

No one "asks" the land how it feels about this, apologizes for the damage, or makes an offering in recompense, as an indigenous person might do. A great deal of energetic turmoil has been released, which will have to be balanced in some way. This is where Distant Healing comes in.

You may feel more inspired to help with some environmental problem you have seen on TV or in the newspapers, which is farther away from home. This is just as important. I emphasize, all through this book, to go with what you are drawn to. This is what you are equipped to deal with; this is your personal challenge.

If you feel drawn to work with environmental issues, your help is certainly needed. Simply attune as usual and set to work in the way you have been practicing so far. By applying the method in the next exercise, you will soon find that you have arrived at a special way of working with the bigger global problems.

---

exercise 39 **RESPONDING TO AN ENVIRONMENTAL ISSUE— SENDING OUT HEALING LIGHT**

- Work on one situation (which has preferably chosen you) or more if you feel inclined. You may need to make a list, just as you did for other subjects. Make sure the phone is disconnected and that you will not be disturbed. Attune your work space and attune yourself, as you have already practiced.

- You may wish to light a candle as a symbol of the Light of the Source. If so, dedicate it to the work and to any helpers you might have in the spiritual realms. Give thanks that you have been given the opportunity to send out healing Light to the environment.

exercise continues >

- Bring your focus to your heart center. As you inhale, visualize this center filling with the Light. With your next breath, the Light fills your chest.

- Allow the particular environmental issue to be brought to mind. You may be surprised by the aspect that is presented to you. Avoid judgment. Ask for the Light to be sent out to the issue you mention. You can say aloud or in your mind, "I ask for healing to be sent to (the presenting issue)."

- If you have a list of issues, ask for the Light to be sent out to each subject as you mention them one by one. Carefully work through your list like this. Take your time. If you feel the need to pause, do so. Pausing simply means that you are in tune with what is happening energetically.

- When you reach the end of your list, give thanks.

- Rest assured that the particular issue, or issues, have received healing that is most needed at this time. Sit quietly with your experience.

- When you have completed your work, blow out the candle. This can be done by sending out the light of the candle. Pause for a moment to see if you intuitively feel where it needs to go. This is usually the first place that comes to mind. As you blow out the candle, say, "I send the Light out to . . . "

- Once you have closed your session, you have handed over the work to higher powers. It is time to stop thinking about it.

In the early stages of practice, alternate the first basic technique of sending out the Light (as above) with the second basic technique of creating the Light pool or circle (Exercise 40).

exercise 40 **RESPONDING TO AN ENVIRONMENTAL ISSUE— CREATING THE LIGHT POOL**

• Work on one situation (which has preferably chosen you) or more if you feel inclined. You may need to make a list, just as you did for other subjects. Make sure the phone is disconnected and that you will not be disturbed. Attune your work space and attune yourself, as you have already practiced.

• You may wish to light a candle as a symbol of the Light of healing. If so, dedicate it to the work and to any helpers you might have in the spiritual realms. Give thanks that you have been given the opportunity to help the environment through the Light of Distant Healing.

• Bring your focus to your heart center. As you inhale, visualize this center filling with Light. With your next breath, the Light fills your chest.

• Now see this Light extending from you to a place in front of you to make an energy pool or circle.

• As you bring your chosen issue to mind, ask for it to be put in the Light. You can say aloud or in your mind: "I ask for healing for (name the issue)." If you have a list of issues, ask for them to be put in the Light, mentioning them one by one. Carefully work through your list like this. Take your time. If you feel the need to pause, do so. Pausing simply means that you are in tune with what is happening energetically.

• Visualize that the issue, or issues, have been gathered into the Light pool or circle. Here they will receive the healing they need most at this time. Sit quietly with your experience.

exercise continues >

- When you have completed your work, give thanks and blow out the candle. This can be done by sending out the light of the candle. Pause for a moment to see if you intuitively feel where it needs to go. This is usually the first place that comes to mind. As you blow out the candle, say, "I send the Light out to . . ."

- Once you have closed your session, you have handed over the work to higher powers. It is time to stop thinking about it.

As before, if you wish to follow a session like this one with some other spiritual practice, you are in the ideal state to do so. If not, realize that the work has opened your energy centers more than is needed for everyday functioning. In other words, you no longer need to be open to that level of energy flow. Carry out the essential Closing-Down Procedure that you learned in Chapter 5.

Some Distant Healers are so sensitive that they absorb incompatible energies from the environmental situations with which they have been working. In this case, the clearing exercise in the Closing-Down Procedure is needed. When your Distant Healing session is in the evening, the Closing-Down Procedure also ensures sound sleep. Remember that "closing down" refers to a procedure that returns your subtle energy system to everyday functioning; it is linked to closing your working sessions. It does not mean fully closing the energy centers or shutting down any of the body systems.

Carrying out the Closing-Down Procedure after each session of work will eventually become second nature. You can also use it to return your subtle energy system to everyday functioning at other times. Even a conversation or reading a book about spiritual or environmental matters can open your centers. This is also what can happen when you work with a group.

Environmental Work with a Group
Group work can be carried out in exactly the same way as set out in Chapter 6 for the Distant Healing Circle in Exercise 19 (page 70) and 20

(page 73). You may even find that the group mixes environmental issues in with other subjects. It is up to the group as a whole to choose how to work. Sometimes a special session devoted exclusively to the environment is a powerful way to highlight the issues in everybody's mind. The energies of the solstices and equinoxes are especially conducive to this form of healing work. Once the program for a session is agreed on, stick to it so that everyone knows what he or she will be doing.

Chapter 12

Working with Plants and Animals

Plants as Teachers and Healers

This is a teaching book, but, as you begin to practice Distant Healing, your experience becomes your own teaching. Teaching comes from within and without. Once you have spent time with the environment, it won't be long before it sends out a challenge to your inner teacher. Are you listening to your inner voice? As sages down the centuries have acknowledged, Nature is our teacher, too.

The fossil record shows that plants were the first to begin colonizing the planet and that this process began in the sea. As we look at the plant world today, we could easily forget the underwater beginning of plants that has ensured their intimate relationship with water. Plants have since formed the nutritional basis for the life of insects and all other animals, including humans. Most plants have the ability to combine the energy of the sun with air, water, and minerals from the Earth to create their stems, leaves, flowers, pollen, fruits, nuts, tubers, roots, which animals, including humans, consume. The plant realm has also provided the basis for the development of pharmaceutical products used in medicine and health care today. But communication with the plants could reveal even more of their healing abilities and intimate structures without our having to dissect them.

Most people's connection with plants is with a garden or window box or by taking a walk in the park. But in the past, we were intimately involved with the plant world, especially during food production. For example, the journey of a loaf of bread to the table began with the sower going out to sow the seed. Then groups of agricultural workers joined in the harvesting by hand, stacking the sheaves of straw and winnowing the grain. This was taken to the mill to be ground into flour and put in sacks. Flour was made available for households or bakers to buy, and the housewife or the baker would make the loaves by hand and bake them. In the developed world, each of these steps in the production of bread has been mechanized, so that many children think that bread is simply something sliced in a packet that you buy in a supermarket. They are totally unaware of how it got there. Where people eat other staple plant foods, there is a similar trend toward mechanization, with a loss of connection with the growing and production process.

The mechanization of food production is undoubtedly a human benefit in many ways, but the intervention of machines affects the food energetically. To test this, hold a pendulum over any food that you have bought, and it will show a negative swing. Or hold your hands over the food, and you will feel your hands sending out energy, often healing energy, to the food product. This means that all those activities where plants come into contact with machines would benefit from Distant Healing.

If we use the road-building scenario, Distant Healing is also needed where plants have been uprooted or destroyed and the energy flow interrupted. Very often you will find that when something destructive happens to plants, the group energy needs healing on behalf of the individuals.

I have a friend who feels pain whenever she sees a truck loaded with felled trees. She senses the effects of the felling and trimming that has not been done in a sacred manner. She feels compelled to send healing to the trees already cut up for transport to the sawmill, as well as the ground where they were once growing and to the other trees left behind.

Your Distant Healing work will always be needed for individual plants, gardens, plantations, and any location where it is necessary to repair the damage caused by local projects. But, as with the mineral environment, there are now global issues that also concern the plant realm. The destruction of the world's rain forests, for example, is already having various catastrophic effects. These vast ecosystems act as the lungs of the planet, giving out oxygen and taking in carbon dioxide.

The overlighting spirits of plant groups have much help to offer us, but, having failed to communicate with them, we are missing these opportunities. However, all is not lost. Distant Healing, which honors and celebrates the plants, will take us all a step forward toward a new and more positive relationship with them. The next two exercises will help you do just that.

---

exercise 41 **ENGAGING WITH THE PLANT WORLD**

You can, of course, commune with plants in pots, even bunches of flowers in a store, but, if possible, go to a place outdoors where there are plants.

- Sit comfortably. Use your breathing to relax your body. Breathe naturally.

- Allow your gaze to relax as you look toward the plants around you. Wait patiently until you feel that a plant, or plants, is calling to you in some way.

- Still relaxed, pay attention to this plant or group of plants. Allow it to "speak" to you. Keep an open mind and suspend your tendency to judgment. Try to simply listen with your full attention.

- When you sense that the communication is over, thank the plants and allow some time to sit with your experience.

- Make a note in your journal. Try the exercise in other locations.

Now we will communicate with a single tree. Trees are beautiful examples of beings, with their heads in the heavens and their roots deep in the soil of the Earth—a lesson in grounding the spiritual in the physical. Some trees are many hundreds of years old and have the wisdom that comes with their great age.

exercise 42 **LISTENING TO A TREE**

Go to a place outdoors where there are trees. They can be any size. Older trees have much to communicate about life on this planet.

- Stand or sit in the landscape. Wait for a tree to "call" to you or focus on one that you feel attracted to. This will happen if you are patient. Either sit close to this tree or stand with your back against it.

- Use your breathing to relax. Wait for the tree to communicate with you.

- Keep an open mind and suspend your tendency to judgment. Try to simply listen with your full attention.

- When you sense that the communication is over, thank the tree and allow some time to sit with your experience.

- Make a note in your journal. Try the exercise with other trees.

This can be a very productive exercise to do with a group, where members can hold hands around the tree. Later, individual experiences can be shared and group learning enhanced. The same applies to the next exercise.

exercise 43 **SENDING DISTANT HEALING TO THE PLANT WORLD**

If you wish to work solo, follow the techniques you have already learned. Here is an example of an advanced technique for when you find yourself working with the plants in a large garden. In such a case, it is important not to decide beforehand what needs your help but to

exercise continues >

go with the flow of the healing. The working scenario would be similar if you were "taken to," say, a large forest.

Though you always work with the subject rather than the condition in astral-level work, you will often be aware of your hands moving into the area of a stated condition, as well as to other important sites. Go with the flow of your guidance and make a note of what happens later.

Note: This exercise is formatted for indoor practice but could just as easily be conducted outside.

- Prepare and dedicate your working space. Make sure that you will not be interrupted in any way. Have your subject, or list of subjects, at hand. Attune, light your candle, and dedicate the work. Ask to be used as a channel for healing and to be guided by your Higher Self (soul). You will look forward to being directed by this source (whether or not you will be doing any Distant Healing at the astral level).

- Sit with your feet flat on the floor or ground with your hands palms up on your thighs or in your lap. The hands should not overlap or touch. (In astral work, it is essential for the palm centers to remain active, hence the palms-up position of the hands.) Use your breath to calm and relax your body. Let go of any worries or anxieties with your out-breath through the open mouth. When you feel attuned, close your mouth and breathe normally. Check that your body is relaxed, including the back of your neck, shoulders, and pelvis. Sit in the silence for a few moments.

- Now put the garden in your mind's eye. Mention it by name, because the vibration of the name strengthens your link (as in the Healing Triangle).

exercise continues >

- Close your eyes to aid concentration. Wait quietly and patiently to see if you become aware that a place in the garden is in front of you. If you have been "taken" to the garden, you will sense this. It becomes easier when you relax and accept that it is possible for this to happen.

- Allow your intuitive guidance to help you sense where your hands need to go.

- If the plant needs healing of any kind, you will feel healing energy leave your hands (or whatever sign tells you that you are working). Keep your hands over the area until you feel a change in the flow of energy, which could be sensed as a marked decrease, or falling off, in intensity. The signal is that all, or part, of the healing is complete.

- As you complete your work with each plant, mentally thank it. Take a full breath and, as you exhale, surround the plant with a protective sphere of light. This may be done mentally or by raising your arms and moving your hands gently to make a sphere around the astral body in front of you.

- Wait for your guidance to see if you need to give healing elsewhere. There may be another plant or plants with which you need to work.

- The energetic activity in your hands is confirmation that this is not taking place in your imagination. A person with developed perceptions would be able to sense or "see" what was going on and confirm that you were working this way.

- When you sense that your work in the garden is complete, relax and allow yourself to return to your physical body.

exercise continues >

- Send out the light of the candle. Pause for a moment to see if you intuitively feel where it needs to go. This is usually the first place that comes to mind. As you blow out the candle, say, "I send the Light out to . . . "

- Carry out the Closing-Down Procedure outlined in Chapter 5.

Group Work with Plants

The needs of the plant realm are an ideal subject for group work. Create your sessions in the usual way. Again, it makes the routine more interesting to have a special session devoted to plants and trees. Similarly, members may come to the meeting one day with particular concerns that they would like the group to address.

Working with the Animal Realm

Animals and plants are constantly caught up in many forms of environmental pollution and devastation: oil and chemical discharge, as well as numerous forms of waste disposal—into the sea, into rivers, and onto land, for example. They also suffer from the destruction and pollution caused by human conflict. Everything that has been said about the environment and plants also applies to the animals. They too experience interruptions to their energy flow, especially on a group basis. Animals are as susceptible to disease and injury as a result of energetic interruption as all other living beings. Many wild animals are under threat of extinction as their habitats become increasingly unviable.

Millions of animals and birds are eaten every year without a sense of gratitude from their human consumers. I recently saw a travel documentary about an idyllic island. The tourists loved to go to the market to buy souvenirs and soak up the atmosphere. In one place, you could buy the freshest chicken, alive in their wooden cages. Seated next to the chickens was a man with a wooden block and a chopper. Once you had ordered your chicken, he would reach into the cage, put the chicken's head on the block, and chop it off in front of the other chickens!

Back home you can see a truck filled with animals bound for the abattoir. There they will line up to be slaughtered, and this will not be done in a sacred manner, with gratitude. Distant Healing is needed in all such situations. Blessing and thanking your food can also become a vital Distant Healing activity.

Animals as Teachers and Healers

On a summer's day in 1995, I found the dead body of a green woodpecker on the doorstep of our house. Marvelling at its beautiful plumage and sorry about its demise, I buried it in the vegetable garden. Later that night, the spirit of the woodpecker communicated with me for more than a half-hour. Woodpecker said that all things had the capacity to teach. As if my chest were the trunk of a tree, Woodpecker bored into it. "You see, I will bore a way through your chest to let the light in and the energy of your heart out!" Was there a link with the green color of its feathers? I wondered. Woodpecker told me how it communes with the trees and understands them.

This knowledge is available to all through communication with Woodpecker. Toward the end of our "conversation," Woodpecker described the meaning of fame: "When you are looked up to, your job is to reflect back the Great Spirit. This is the only purpose of being looked up to, so that you send back the image of spiritual truth."

Two years later, I received an intriguing message from a particular magpie that lives with its family in a pine near my home. The message was about how love was carried by the birds in color and sound. Even a lowly fly once told me some dazzling stories about multiple sight. The wonder of all the communications I have received from the animal realm is that they seem totally relevant to everyone's life, yet they were couched in a way that also had personal significance for me. This is why I encourage you to commune with the animals. Doing so will also greatly enhance your work with them as a Distant Healer. Many owners tell of conversations with their pets and how their pets often seem to know their innermost thoughts. Although you may have an animal you are fond of, the next exercise needs to be with an animal you have never met.

exercise 44 COMMUNING WITH THE ANIMAL REALM

- Go somewhere outdoors where you can sit comfortably. Take a few full breaths to help you relax your body. The object of the exercise is to be fully relaxed, while at the same time being fully aware.

- Now attune to what is before you. This means putting your mind in the heart center while you allow your relaxed gaze to look into the distance. Also become aware of what is nearby.

- Pay attention to stillness, birdsong, rustlings, and movement; to the feel of the air and the feeling of the day; and so on.

- If you live in an urban setting, you can train yourself to hear beyond the sounds of traffic.

- Close your eyes and listen. What do you hear?

- Allow yourself to "hear" the voice of an animal or bird in your environment. Be patient, in active waiting mode (the opposite of just passing the time).

- This is a way of honoring the animal life around you. It deepens your perception of, and alignment with, the animals on all levels. Before leaving, give your thanks.

Regular practice of this exercise will reveal many life secrets. Make a note of your experience in your journal. You can decide whether it is appropriate for you to share it with other people or your Distant Healing group. When you can, sharing is always a way of learning.

Domestic Animals and Pets

Like all life forms, animals respond to love and lovelessness. All animals are sensitive to their owner's state of health and well-being, because they are able to pick this up on all levels. As with human situations, there are a number of occasions when Distant Healing is appropriate and ideal for animal subjects. For example, some animals may be too dangerous to approach, because they are wild, their injury prevents contact, or they are inaccessible.

You may get requests to send healing to domestic animals and pets in the same way as you would for human subjects. In some countries, the treatment of animals is the sole preserve of veterinary surgeons, so hands-on healing is only practiced with the full permission of the vet. There are, however, no such restrictions for Distant Healers. Send your healing help just as you did in the baseline exercises of Chapter 5.

When you receive a request to send healing to a sick animal, you may find that you are called upon to wait to see if you are going to work on the astral level. If so, your work may proceed along the lines of the following exercise.

---

exercise 45 **WORKING WITH A SICK ANIMAL— ASTRAL-LEVEL HEALING**

Animals are very open and receptive to this form of healing. Though you always work with the subject, rather than the condition, in astral-level work, you will often be aware of your hands moving into the area of a stated condition, as well as to other important sites, such as the centers. Go with the flow of your guidance and make a note of what happens later.

- Make sure that you will not be interrupted in any way. Prepare and dedicate your working space. Have your list of subjects at hand. Attune, light your candle, and dedicate the work. Ask to be used as a channel for healing and to be guided by your Higher Self (soul).

exercise continues >

You will look forward to being directed by this source (whether or not you will be doing any Distant Healing at the astral level).

- Sit with your feet flat on the floor with your hands palms up on your thighs or in your lap. The hands should not overlap or touch. (In astral work, it is essential for the palm centers to remain active, hence the palms-up position of the hands.)

- Use your breath to calm and relax your body. Let go of any worries or anxieties with your out-breath through the open mouth. When you feel attuned, close your mouth and breathe normally. Check that your body is relaxed, including the back of your neck, shoulders, and pelvis. Sit in the silence for a few moments.

- Now focus on the request for help. Mention the subject by name (if the animal has one), because the vibration of the name strengthens your link with the animal (as in the Healing Triangle, see Figure 1, page 13).

- Close your eyes to aid with concentration. Wait quietly and patiently to see if you become aware that the subject is in front of you.

- If you have been "taken" to the animal or it has been "brought" to you, you will sense the animal's presence. This becomes easier when you relax and accept that it is possible for this to happen. You will also be able to sense whether the animal is lying or sitting in front of you and how the body is orientated.

- Mentally make sure that you are comfortably oriented to carry out what needs to be done. Allow your intuitive guidance to help you sense where your hands need to go.

exercise continues >

- Let's take an example as illustration: Your help has been requested for a cat that has become ill. In this case, once you are aware of the cat's astral body in front of you, you will probably feel drawn to put your hands over the area in question. If this is what it needs, you will feel healing energy leave your hands, or whatever sign tells you that you are working. Keep your hands over the area until you feel a change in the flow of energy, which could be sensed as a marked decrease, or falling off, in intensity. This signals that all, or part, of the healing is complete.

- Wait for your guidance to see if you need to give healing elsewhere. There may be a center involved, for example, or you may need to move your hands to somewhere else.

- The energetic activity in your hands is confirmation that this is not taking place in your imagination. A person with developed perceptions would be able to sense or "see" what was going on and confirm that you were working on the astral level.

- When you have completed your work, mentally thank the animal. Now take a full breath and, as you exhale, surround the animal with a protective sphere of light. This may be done mentally or by raising your arms and moving your hands gently to make a sphere around the astral body in front of you (as in Figure 21, page 130).

- At this point, either the animal returns to its physical body or you return to your physical body. (When there is another subject to work with, you may also remain in the astral-body state to receive the next subject on your list in the same way.)

exercise continues >

- If there is another subject to work with, first make sure that the one you were working on is no longer in front of you (it has returned to its physical body). Now visualize clearing, silver light washing over your upraised palms. You can then proceed to the next subject on your list. Take a short pause if you feel the need.

- Follow the same procedure as before. Break your link with the last subject by clearing your hands.

- When you have completed your work, blow out the candle. This can be done by sending out the light of the candle. Pause for a moment to see if you intuitively feel where the Light should be sent. This is usually the first place that comes to mind. As you blow out the candle, say, "I send the Light out to . . . "

- Carry out the Closing-Down Procedure outlined in Chapter 5.

The Death of an Animal

A common situation where Distant Healing is called for occurs when a pet animal is dying or passing over. Sadness and a sense of loss surround the passing of a pet. However, in terms of a life journey, the animal, just like a human person, is dropping off the body and continuing life without it—continuing the life that was there before the body.

The Distant Healer is joining the animal on this part of its journey, so the request for help over a passing or terminal illness is an honor. Distant Healing also helps the veterinary team that has the job of putting the animal down. Finally, healing should be sent to the owner who is going to suffer distress at the death of the animal. This is the subject of the next exercise.

If you find that you are affected by cases like these, you will find help by reviewing Chapter 9 again.

exercise 46 **SENDING HEALING TO A DYING ANIMAL**

In this scenario, you have been told that a friend's dog is very sick and cannot benefit from further treatment. In order to end its suffering, it is going to be put down. The friend asks you to send healing.

- Make sure the phone is disconnected and that you will not be disturbed. Attune both your work space and yourself.

- You may wish to light a candle as a symbol of the Light of healing. If so, dedicate it to the work and any helpers you might have in the spiritual realms. Give thanks that you have been given the opportunity to send out healing Light.

- Bring your focus to your heart center. As you inhale, visualize this center filling with the Light. With the next breath, the Light fills your chest.

- Ask for the Light to be sent out to the dog. You can say aloud or in your mind, "I ask for healing to be sent to (name)." Offer your thanks.

- When you have a list of animal subjects, carefully work through your list. Take your time. If you feel the need to pause, do so. Pausing simply means that you are in tune with what is happening energetically. When you reach the end of your list, give thanks.

- Rest assured that healing Light has been sent to where it is needed. Sit quietly with your experience.

- When you have completed your work, blow out the candle. This can be done by sending out the light of the candle. Pause for a

exercise continues >

moment to see if you intuitively feel where the Light should be sent. As you blow out the candle, say, "I send the Light out to . . ."

- Once you have closed your session, you have handed the list to higher powers. It is time to stop thinking about the case.

Don't forget your Closing-Down Procedure, Chapter 5.

You could alternate similar cases with the Light pool technique below.

exercise 47 **CREATING THE LIGHT POOL FOR A DYING ANIMAL**
In this case, you have been contacted by someone at a racecourse. A horse has had a serious accident and must be put down. Allow your intuition to help you create a list of subjects, beginning with the horse. You might want to include the rider, the owner, and all those who witnessed the accident and subsequent injury to the horse.

- Make sure the phone is disconnected and that you will not be disturbed. Attune your work space and yourself.

- You may wish to light a candle as a symbol of the Light of healing. If so, dedicate it to the work and any helpers you might have in the spiritual realms. Give thanks that you have been given the opportunity to help others through the Light of Distant Healing.

- Bring your focus to your heart center. As you inhale, visualize this center filling with Light. With the next breath, the Light fills your chest.

- Now see this Light extending from you to a place in front of you to make an energy pool or circle.

exercise continues >

- As you look over your list, ask for those on it to be put in the Light, mentioning them one by one. You can say this aloud or in your mind, "I ask for healing for (name)."

- Carefully work through your list. Take your time, pausing if necessary. Pausing simply means that you are in tune with what is happening energetically.

- When you reach the end of your list, give thanks.

- Visualize that all those on the list have been gathered into the Light pool or circle, where they will receive the healing they need. Sit quietly with your experience.

- When you have completed your work, blow out the candle. This can be done by sending out the light of the candle. Pause for a moment to see if you intuitively feel where the Light should be sent. As you blow out the candle, say, "I send the Light out to . . . "

Once you have closed your session, you have handed the list to higher powers. It is time to stop thinking about the case.

Honoring Your Work

You will have found that animals, plants, and the landscape are gateways to other states of consciousness. Their teaching is that they are copartners with us in shaping the living environment. Careful study of your journal entries may show an emerging pattern of work that demonstrates your unique affinity with certain aspects of the Earth and/or the Earth family. If you work with a Distant Healing group, a way of honoring the work can be a way for each member to tell his or her Earth story.

exercise 48 **TELLING YOUR EARTH STORY**

- After your Distant Healing work, break up into groups of three or four.

- When it is your turn, tell the small group about a particular life experience in which you felt the presence of the natural world.

- Some members have felt pain over what is befalling the planet and its natural inhabitants. In the words of the celebrated Vietnamese Zen master Thich Nhat Hanh, they have "heard the Earth crying."

- Listen to each account with compassion and full attention, watching for signs of your own "tuning out."

- Let silence surround each Earth story.

- Recreate the circle and pass the Love around to end the session.

To deal with the second of the two crucial issues of our time, we are certainly going to need some unconditional love. But the most empowering thing for us, as Distant Healers, is that we can beam this healing Love into those violent situations and to the family, societal, political, and economic issues that are crying out for help in every part of our planet. In the next chapter, we will look at how to set about doing this.

Chapter 13

Taking Action to Heal Local and Global Issues

The Polarization of Human Behavior

As far as the natural world is concerned, the raising of human consciousness cannot happen soon enough. However, as the pressure for change increases, it is tending to polarize people. Some are becoming more spiritually aware and want to implement lifestyle choices accordingly, whereas the responses of others range from the apathetic and despairing to the violent and chaotic. We are witnessing this polar reaction now, and it is creating important new challenges for Distant Healing.

Somewhere in the middle of the two poles of consciousness is a general feeling of separation. This is the destructive expansion of the sense of separation from others and the natural world. People no longer feel part of a family, of a network of friends, of a community, or of a nation, and few have ever considered themselves as part of the global community.

Many human activities encourage separation, especially those of political, religious, nationalistic, and ethnic groups. Nearer to home, we are separated by lifestyle, income, gender, sexuality, age, disability, and the way we appear to others. The media constantly reports on the impact of these divisions, so that they are further imprinted on our minds. Our Oneness with one another should mean that we enjoy and celebrate difference. Instead, difference is used to encourage one group to feel superior to another and to provide the excuse to denigrate and exploit others. Very often these conditioned attitudes are backed by so-called sacred texts or traditional cultural norms, making communication nearly impossible or very difficult.

One of the problems with polarization is that it becomes the great divide, with each polarity fearing and hating the other and wanting to further emphasize difference rather than reaching out with compassion and understanding. The energetic problem is even deeper. As with the effects of disruption on the natural world, polarization among human beings is creating serious interruptions to energy flow. This, in turn, creates a chronic malaise in the global population, which manifests as disease, despair, fear, and violence. These effects are mirrored in environmental problems, such as drought, famine, earthquake, destructive climate change, and so on.

The Challenge for Distant Healers

Our own sense of helplessness often stems from feelings that the things we hear about are always beyond our control—a war-torn country, extreme cruelty meted out to the innocent, a frightening mechanical disaster—because they are happening in other parts of the world. But sooner or later the repercussions of these happenings will come knocking on our door, and we will ignore them at our peril. Years ago it was happening to *them*, and they were far away. But now it is happening in our neighborhood.

We know all about these things because the media is very good at reporting them. Nevertheless, as Distant Healers, we want to do something. After all, what is the point of helping the people on our healing list if we do nothing to help those bruised and battered societies in which they and others live? Those societies are part of our world, too. Distant Healing offers everyone in every society the opportunity to become empowered.

The Network of Consciousness

Quantum mechanics scientists believe that the unified field theory connects everything in the universe, including gravity, nuclear reactions, electromagnetic forces, and human consciousness. Modern physics, then, supports the findings of Distant Healing that thought forms, such as ideas and information, are able to travel from one part of the human family to another via a network of consciousness (the unified field of science). This theory explains how negative thoughts and information are having such a disastrous effect on the human psyche; it is also the clue to positive action. The network of consciousness operates unconditionally, and energetic transactions move in all directions. Recall that the network of consciousness facilitates your being able to send healing Light to anywhere in the universe. We can take good advantage of this in planning how to use Distant Healing to heal the effects of fear and hatred.

The Plan of Action

I suggest that you begin with a twofold plan. First, start with your own locality. Send out healing Light into it or send it out to specific local needs. Second, keep the big picture in mind by simply observing what is going on, without judgment and without thinking about how a certain problem should be solved. This is the same attitude you used in your Distant Healing practice, when I encouraged you to be open to the guidance of your intuition, or Higher Self.

Allow a situation to call to you, just as you did with elements of the landscape, the plants, and the animals. When you become aware of this call, it is because you are equipped to deal with the situation at that point in time and your healing contribution is needed. The exercises that follow are suggestions for practice and should be modified to suit your own, or your group's, needs.

---

exercise 49 **SENDING LIGHT INTO A LOCALITY**

First decide how you feel and think about the situation with which you want to work. Use your breathing to calm and relax yourself. Your healing request should be unconditional. Do not decide in advance what you think should happen in this locality. Instead allow decisions to be made at the level of the Higher Self. Remember, healing energy, like prayer, travels at the level of intentional thought.

exercise continues >

- Make sure the phone is disconnected and that you will not be disturbed. Attune both your work space and yourself.

- You may wish to light a candle as a symbol of the Light of the Source. If so, dedicate it to the work and to any helpers you might have in the spiritual realms. Give thanks that you have been given the opportunity to send out healing Light.

- Bring your focus to your heart center. As you inhale, visualize this center filling with the Light. With your next breath, the Light fills your chest.

- Ask for the Light to be sent out to the locality you specify. You can say aloud or in your mind: "I ask for healing to be sent to (name)."

- If you are sending out to more than one locality, ask for the Light to be sent out to each locality as you mention them one by one. Carefully work through your list, taking your time and pausing if necessary. Pausing means that you are in tune with what is happening energetically.

- When you reach the end of your list, give thanks. Sit quietly with your experience.

- Rest assured that healing Light has been sent to where it is needed.

- When you have completed your work, blow out the candle. This can be done by sending out the light of the candle. Pause for a moment to see if you intuitively feel where it needs to go. As you blow out the candle, say, "I send the Light out to . . . "

- Once you have closed your session, relax and realize that you have handed over the situation(s) to higher powers.

exercise 50 **SENDING LIGHT TO A DISASTER SITUATION—
THE DISTANT HEALING CIRCLE**

Your group has agreed that if there is a report of a disaster or situation
that they would like to address, then they will focus the session on it.
In this case, the situation was reported on TV that day.

figure 24 **A Disaster Situation**

• Disconnect all telephones. Arrange the chairs in a circle with a
  small table in the center with a candle and some matches. Members
  might like to add items symbolizing healing. When possible, the
  group should sit with male next to female and experienced next to
  inexperienced. By alternating genders and experience levels, the
  energies of the Circle are easier to balance.

• The chosen leader should open the meeting with a welcome and
  should help the group to attune. He or she then facilitates the
  Distant Healing.

exercise continues >

- The leader's role is to make sure that everyone is in the best possible state to work. It may be necessary, therefore, for the group to first discuss the report. Covering various aspects of the report in discussion helps the group focus on it.

- The group sits in a circle with feet flat on the floor and hands palms up on their thighs or in their laps, without linking.

- The leader instructs the group as follows: "Take six breaths to calm and relax your body, letting go of any worries or anxieties with your out-breath, through the open mouth. When you feel attuned, close the mouth and breathe normally.

- "Check that your body is relaxed, including the back of your neck, shoulders, and pelvis. Close your eyes and allow the calm silence to settle."

- The leader lights the candle and dedicates the light to the work of the Circle, asking for protection and soul guidance.

- The leader continues: "The light of the candle is the Light of the Source of healing. Breathe it into the heart center. Allow the Light to fill your chest.

- "Now pass the energy in your heart center to the person on your left, so that we are all linked together." Intuitively, you may have to wait a moment to gather your heart energy before you can pass on.

- The leader should be aware of the need for a pause and should allow enough time for group linking, as this is the foundation of

exercise continues >

the Circle. With practice, it is possible to sense when energetic linking is complete.

- With the Circle ready, the leader expresses the purpose of the meeting and gives thanks, on behalf of the group, for the opportunity to be of service. The group healing request should be unconditional. This allows decisions about outcomes to be made at the level of the Higher Self. Remember, healing energy, like prayer, travels at the level of the intentional thought.

- With this in mind, the leader asks for healing Light to be sent to the situation. A simple form of this could be, "We ask for healing to be sent to (state the situation without adding opinions or judgment)."

- The group sits together in silence. It is important to realize that the group's intention, motivated by love, has enabled the Light of healing to be sent to the situation.

- The leader gives time for quiet reflection and then indicates that the sending-out process is complete with a verbal signal, such as "Thank you."

- After a short break, the group can discuss the work of the Circle by sharing experiences and queries to consolidate learning.

- The work may be followed by another spiritual activity, such as meditating, giving a reading, or listening to music.

- Finally, the leader closes the Healing Circle. As the candle is blown out, the Light can be sent out to where it is needed, as when working alone.

exercise continues >

- Before closing the meeting, the group should carry out the Closing-Down Procedure from Chapter 5. This could be led by the chosen leader.

The reflection time can be used to make notes or to illustrate the experience in some way. It allows the group to log their experience and learning, chart the energies they have been working with, and ground the experience, giving the mind time to absorb what has happened.

Working with the Injured and Dying

You have heard a news item about the dire situation of people in a certain war zone. When this item comes up on TV, there are close-up pictures of the injured, including women and children. These scenes become imprinted on your mind. You decide that you will include them in your next Distant Healing session. You make sure that you will be able to maintain a calm state and that you will be able to work unconditionally. When you sit to work and find yourself needing to send healing in the advanced (astral) way, your session could proceed as in the following exercise.

exercise 51 SENDING OUT TO THE INJURED AND DYING —ASTRAL-LEVEL HEALING

First check your mental and emotional response to the situation. Your healing request should be unconditional. Do not decide in advance what you think should happen. Allow decisions to be made at the level of the Higher Self. Remember, healing energy, like prayer, travels at the level of the intentional thought.

Healing Light will always help the dying to pass over. As with earlier situations, this Light will also be needed by the rescue team and those

exercise continues >

who were witnesses to what happened. So be prepared to go with the flow of your guidance and make a note of your experience later.

- Make sure that you will not be interrupted in any way. Prepare and dedicate your working space. Attune yourself, light your candle, and dedicate the work. Ask to be used as a channel for healing and to be guided by your Higher Self (soul). You will look forward to being directed by this source (whether or not you will be doing any Distant Healing at the astral level).

- Sit with your feet flat on the floor with your hands palms up on your thighs or in your lap. The hands should not overlap or touch. (In astral work, it is essential for the palm centers to remain active, hence the palms-up position of the hands.) Use your breath to calm and relax your body. Let go of any worries or anxieties with your out-breath through the open mouth. When you feel attuned, close your mouth and breathe normally. Check that your body is relaxed, including the back of your neck, shoulders, and pelvis. Sit in the silence for a few moments.

- Close your eyes to aid with concentration. Allow the faces and bodies of the dead and injured to come to mind again. Check that you can make your request without adding your own opinions or judgments.

- Wait quietly and patiently to see if you become aware that a subject is in front of you.

- If you have been "taken" to the person or the person has been "brought" to you, you will sense his or her presence. This becomes easier when you relax and accept that it is possible for this to

exercise continues >

happen. You will also be able to sense whether the adult person, child, or baby is lying or sitting in front of you and how the body is orientated.

- Mentally make sure that you are comfortably orientated to carry out what needs to be done. Allow your intuitive guidance to help you sense where your hands need to go.

- If this is what is needed, you will feel healing energy leave your hands, or whatever sign tells you that you are working. Keep your hands in the same position until you feel a change in the flow of energy, which could be sensed as a marked decrease, or falling off, in intensity. This signals that all, or part, of the healing is complete.

- Wait for your guidance to see if you need to give healing elsewhere. The energetic activity in your hands is confirmation that this is not taking place in your imagination. A person with developed perceptions would be able to sense or "see" what was going on and confirm that you were working this way.

- When you have completed your work with the subject, mentally thank him or her. Take a full breath and, as you exhale, surround the person with a protective sphere of light. This may be done mentally or by raising your arms and moving your hands gently to make a sphere around the astral body in front of you (Figure 21, page 130).

- When there is another subject to work with, first make sure that the one you were working on is no longer in front of you. Visualize clearing, silver light washing over your upraised palms.

exercise continues >

You can now proceed to the next subject. Take a short pause if you feel the need.

• Follow the same procedure as before. Break your link with the last subject by clearing your hands.

• When you have completed your work, blow out the candle. This can be done by sending out the light of the candle. Pause for a moment to see if you intuitively feel where the Light should be sent. As you blow out the candle, say, "I send the Light out to . . . "

• Carry out the Closing-Down Procedure outlined in Chapter 5.

If during an astral-level healing you sense that you are no longer sitting in your chair, but standing over or by the subject, you will know that you have traveled to them. Stay relaxed and proceed as described. You are quite safe, and you can move out of this state whenever you like.

This way of working requires intense, but relaxed, concentration. Therefore, I recommend that you start working with one subject at a time, with an aim of no more than six in any one session, unless guided otherwise. You need to feel totally comfortable and build up your confidence so that you do not get tired by the level of focused effort needed to work this way. In the case above, I assume that you have achieved this level of confidence. Keep a note of what happens in your journal.

By the time you have used both baseline and advanced techniques with the second group of the crucial world issues, you may feel that the work resonates for you in a special way. Perhaps you would like to specialize in this area. Your Distant Healing journal will give you clues about this.

By now, you have discovered that there is a great deal of work to be done in this field and in all the other fields of work that we have covered on your healing journey. Life presents us with many difficult and scary situations, but, in the midst of them, and surrounding them, is the eternal beauty of the world. Humor, courage, and determination accentuate the positive. Remember to look for the Light; there are always moments of wonder.

On this journey, you are responsible for you. Distant Healing emphasizes that there are two sides to life, not just the negative side. Take steps to keep your life in balance. It is important to look after yourself, to keep yourself well, to enjoy life. This will ensure that you keep your healing channel open and in prime condition. In the final chapter, we will look at how to do this. All good endings have a surprise—and I have one for you.

part four

Chapter 14

A Way of Being

The Heart Center—Taking Care of the Divine Dream

In this final chapter, we revisit the heart center. Distant Healing begins in this center, because it is the focal point of the divine dream of incarnation, of the total human being. As we near the end of our work together, this may seem obvious. But how our incarnation through the heart center came about is one of the wonders of the human being.

Human birth is the grounding of the divine dream, the earthing of the Light of Oneness. We know that living beings, the planet, and the cosmos on which they depend are facets of Oneness. Because Oneness means that if any part of the whole is suffering then every part experiences that suffering, to take care of the divine dream is a responsibility that is at the core of the Distant Healing agenda.

With their understanding of spiritual reality, indigenous and shamanic peoples have always accepted that restoring balance and harmony at the subtle levels is as necessary as restoring physical health and well-being. Distant Healing moves between both of these worlds, as well as being in them, and so complements (and is not an alternative to) allopathic medicine and all therapeutic practice, because it operates on all levels of our being.

The Creative Role of the Heart Center

In Chapter 3, I described how the Light beings that we are need a series of vehicles, or "bodies," in order to travel on the various levels, culminating in the physical body. The heart center plays a crucial role in this embodiment process.

Once the spiritual intention has been put in place, the physical body is prepared through the activation of the etheric template. As the incoming spiritual force moves toward physicality, it first becomes embodied in a spirit body. The energy of the spirit body moves to meet the incoming spiritual force, and the two merge in what we know as the heart center. The spirit body, with its heart center, is the soul or Higher Self. From here, the spiritual force takes on a number of other bodies, or vibrating patterns of energy. Spirit has become embodied at a mental, emotional, etheric, and physical level. Each energy pattern is vibrating at a rate lower than the incoming spiritual force, becoming progressively slower until the physical level is reached. At each stage of embodiment, the energy of the next "body" merges with the spiritual force in the heart center. Thus, the heart center is where we hear the voice of the Higher Self, often in the form of feelings.

Maintaining the Channel

Maintaining your own healing channel is the same thing as understanding and maintaining your heart center. When the focus of your attunement is the heart center, it ensures that you engage with the indwelling spiritual force, and your mental and emotional intention is sent out at this level. Looking after your heart center, then, is the key to maintaining your healing channel.

Once a week, look into your heart center in a calm, observant way. Acknowledging that this is the place of the soul, ask yourself if your heart center is a combination of serene temple and lively workshop, or is it a place of confinement and frustration? Perhaps you have a sense already, but you can make an accurate assessment with the next exercise.

exercise 52 ASSESSING THE STATE OF THE HEART CENTER

- Sit quietly where you will not be disturbed. Put one hand over your heart center. Does it feel warm or cold, soft or hard, alive or struggling to live?

- Imagine that you can see into your heart center. Visualize its two equal halves, each with two chambers, somewhat like your physical heart. The left half receives energy, receives life; the right half gives out energy, gives out to life.

- You need to have a fully functioning heart. Take a look at the left half. Ask your heart center, How am I closed to receiving love? Wait for the response.

- To be fully receptive, you need to be open to life, to feel good about yourself, and to feel clear about your choices. When you feel closed, defensive, and wanting to avoid painful situations or to be protected from them, you need to loosen up and discover what really matters to you. When difficulties come your way, the first step is to accept them. You will be able to use Distant Healing as your next step.

- When you feel indifferent about things, full of doubts, and unable to make choices, the receptive half of your heart center is asking you to conserve energy, gather your strength, and wait patiently for clarity and inspiration. Recognize these energies when they appear so that you can receive them.

- Now look at the right half of your heart center. Ask your heart center, How do I stop myself from giving love? Wait for the response.

exercise continues >

• To be fully able to give out energy as a healing and vitalizing force, you need to be able to sense the inner strength that makes you wholehearted in what you do. When you feel half-hearted and apathetic, you are in the wrong place. This could be the wrong physical, emotional, mental, or spiritual place, or a combination of them. It's time to remove yourself from the situation. Patiently hold on to your own space until you feel the energies of interest and excitement returning.

• When you realize that you are not being authentic, not being the real you, you have uncovered a lack of courage (the power of the heart, which is actually a form of love). Again, look into yourself and decide what really matters to you, what seems to have "heart." Take charge of your energies and put what has heart back into your life. This will unlock courage and the ability to give and receive love.

Each of the exercises that follow help toward your goal of achieving a fully functioning heart center and of maintaining the healing channel.

exercise 53 **HEART CENTER BREATHING**

This exercise is excellent for balancing and revitalizing the system, especially when working from the heart center as in Distant Healing.

• Sit comfortably with your feet flat on the ground. Rest your hands on your thighs, palms up (in receptive mode). Breathe normally. Relax your elbows, the back of your neck, and the tops of your shoulders. Do this by "letting go" with each out-breath. Close your eyes if this helps you to concentrate.

exercise continues >

- Breathe into the heart center. As you do so, visualize a green light in your heart center that gets brighter each time you inhale. Allow the green light to fill up the heart center and move out into the area of the body around it.

- Let your focus move slowly and gently down to the solar plexus center. Visualize a golden yellow light as you inhale. Allow this light to fill up the center and the area of the body around it.

- Now let your focus move slowly and gently down to the sacral center. Visualize a bright orange light as you inhale. Allow this light to fill up the center and the area of the body around it.

- Let your focus move slowly and gently down to the base center. Visualize a bright red light as you inhale. Allow this light to fill up the center and the area of the body around it.

- Return your focus to the heart center. See the green light awaiting you. Let your focus slowly and gently rise to the throat center. Visualize a sky-blue light as you inhale. Allow this light to fill up the center and the areas of the throat, nose, and ears.

- Let your focus slowly and gently rise to the brow center. Visualize a royal-blue or indigo light as you inhale. Allow this light to fill up the center and the head and eyes.

- Let your focus slowly and gently rise to the crown center. Visualize a violet light as you inhale. Allow this light to fill up the center and cover the top of the head.

- Return your focus to the heart center. Visualize the green light awaiting you again. Relax and breathe naturally.

exercise continues >

This exercise is an excellent antidote to the effects of negative information on the centers (as described in Chapter 9).

The heart center is the place of balance for the seven main subtle energy centers. As well as reminding us that our core is the Higher Self, the heart center is able to bring balance to all the levels of our being. Next is a simple exercise in which the heart center plays the role of balancing the body energies.

exercise 54 **BALANCING BODY ENERGIES**

This exercise can be done anywhere, as long as you have a place to lie down. As well as balancing the body energies, this exercise relaxes and refreshes the system.

- Loosen your clothing and make sure there is no constriction around your neck. Lie down in a firm, comfortable place, with the head supported. The legs should be a little apart, with the arms by the sides of the body.

- Take three full breaths, letting go of tension as you exhale. Breathe naturally and "let go" of the body. Focus on the heart center with your eyes open.

- Remain relaxed but alert, without allowing yourself to drift off. Let your body find its own relaxed position. Listen to the body as it finds its own balance. Notice how areas of tension relax. Some of your limbs may move slightly.

- Maintain your focus on the heart center.

exercise continues >

- After about fifteen minutes, the body's energies will become balanced. When this occurs, a tingling sensation or feeling of internal lightness may be sensed all over the body. Remain lying in this position for as long as you need to.

- You will feel refreshed. Before getting up, give thanks for the body's ability to refresh itself in this way.

Greeting the Day

Keeping your healing channel open means being conscious of your alignment with the sacred. You can make this balancing exercise a part of your daily routine. There are numerous ways of starting the day with this in mind. I like to start my day by acknowledging the sun as a symbol of the Light. The next exercise promotes your sensitivity to the natural cycles of giving and receiving.

The seven breaths of greeting symbolize the seven directions of east, south, west, north, above, below, and within.

exercise 55 **THE SEVEN BREATHS OF GREETING**
If possible, practice this exercise outside.

- Face the direction of the dawn, the place of the rising sun, standing or sitting. Use your breath to relax the body. Become aware of your feet and their contact with the ground. Feel your connection to the Earth.

- Give thanks for the previous night. Be aware that the source of energy, and the promise of each day, is within you.

exercise continues >

- Feel the air around you. Become aware of your breath and the fresh air entering your nostrils and your lungs. Note how your whole body enjoys the breath of the new day.

- As you breathe slowly and naturally, raise your arms as if you were lifting them up to the sun.

- In this position of thanks and greeting, take seven deep breaths down into the abdomen. As you inhale, visualize the life force in the air moving into the various parts of your body and your energy field.

- With the first breath, visualize the life force moving down the length of your spine, filling it with life and relaxing the muscles of your back.

- With the second breath, take the life force down into your pelvis and legs, allowing it to relax the muscles of this region.

- With the third breath, take the life force into the shoulders and arms, allowing it to relax the muscles.

- With the fourth breath, let the life force fill the head and neck, relaxing the neck.

- With the fifth breath, let the life force fill the organs of the abdomen, relaxing the abdominal muscles.

- With the sixth breath, let the life force fill the chest and heart center, relaxing the muscles of the chest.

exercise continues >

- With the seventh breath, let the life force fill your whole energy field, harmonizing and balancing the energies within it.

- Enjoy this state of harmony for a few moments before moving off.

You can vary how you direct the seven breaths, according to your needs on any particular day. For example, you may need to focus more energy on a specific part of the body. If you are able to practice the exercise outside, notice the world around you as you calmly take your breaths. Feel your sacred connection with life being renewed. Acknowledge the other life forms that may be present.

Honoring Food

Communicating with your body about food can be a revelation. We rarely ask our bodies what they *need*, and we demand that they cope with what we want, when and how we want it. We are not concerned with how our bodies feel when we rush to eat or when we eat without caring what we put in our mouth. The next meal may be the right time to communicate with your body.

Because your food has been part of a living plant or animal, handled by different people and machinery, transported and packaged, it contains a range of vibrations, some of which are not compatible with yours. Blessing your food thanks it, clears it, and brings its energies into alignment with your own. Using your hands in a sacred manner to bless food enhances the subtle energy structures of the palms.

exercise 56 **BLESSING AND THANKING FOOD**

- When you are going to eat or drink something, first hold your hands over it to see if your body really needs it. If you sense that it

exercise continues >

does not, honor your intuitive awareness and the body's friendly message by not consuming it. Of course, this process should ideally begin in the shop!

• All food and drink can be honored through your remembrance of the hand-heart link. Use your hands to bless and thank your food and drink before consuming them.

Mealtimes should always be harmonious. Your body will tell you that food should always be eaten with enjoyment and never with anxiety about what it is made of, and so on. Blessing your food has taken care of this, so go ahead and enjoy your food as a gift from the planet. Thank those who grow and prepare it for you, as well as those working in factories where the meal has been manufactured (when this is the case).

Getting together, celebrating, and eating with others are wonderful ways of sharing food. When you have reached this point in the book, why not celebrate your achievement with a party!

Distant Healing Support Energies—The Third Challenge

Distant Healing emphasizes the positive while working with the negative. Your journey with this book has shown you the huge variety of situations that need the benefits of healing. But you will also have noticed how an important aspect of Distant Healing is its supportive role.

My surprise for you is that we can go further in this supportive role, that there is actually a third challenge for Distant Healers today: to send out to those people and organizations that are doing constructive work for the whole—whether human, animal, plant, or environment—and to situations where these positive activities are taking place. As it does for the teams involved in rescue and care, the energy of Love will help and support, as well as heal. The positive energy field that you will help to create around those people and situations will attract what is needed. As in all your work, Distant Healing support energies must be sent unconditionally. You do not need to decide what are the "good" things and who are the most "deserving."

An attitude of openheartedness is ensured by your being aware of what comes into your orbit, of what is presented to you, because you are the person to deal with it. Life is coming toward you every moment. Be receptive and take it as it comes, giving thanks for it. Giving thanks completes the energy circle.

To get used to working with this third challenge, let's take a typical example, which is one of many possibilities.

exercise 57 **SENDING OUT TO A PROJECT**

You hear about a certain project that is doing work to help underprivileged people. The project resonates with you, and you would like to send out Distant Healing support energies.

- Make sure the phone is disconnected and that you will not be disturbed. Attune both your work space and yourself.

- You may wish to light a candle as a symbol of the Light of the Source. If so, dedicate it to the work and to any helpers you might have in the spiritual realms. Give thanks that you have been given the opportunity to send out the Light of support.

- Bring your focus to your heart center. As you inhale, visualize this center filling with the Light. With your next breath, the Light fills your chest.

- Ask for the Light to be sent out to the project you have in mind. You can say aloud or in your mind, "I ask for support to be sent to (name the project and all those working for it)."

- Give thanks and rest assured that the project and project workers have received the Distant Healing support energies they need. Sit quietly with your experience.

exercise continues >

- When you have completed your work, blow out the candle. This can be done by sending out the light of the candle. Pause for a moment to see if you intuitively feel where it needs to go. This is usually the first thing that comes to mind. As you blow out the candle, you could say, "I send the Light out to all that is beautiful in our world."

- Once you have closed your session, you have handed over the list to higher powers.

By now, you won't be surprised if exercises like that take you into advanced-level mode, if this is what is needed. Go with the flow of the energies. Practice will soon get you used to the idea that you can send support and goodwill as easily as you can send healing help.

The group scenario will be very similar to the one you have already practiced. If the group agrees, Distant Healing support can be part of your work together. Attunement and your focus in the heart center will always honor the fact that Love is unconditional.

Being Aware of Beauty

Beauty tells us about soul. Our connection to beauty nourishes us at a deep level. Take time to notice the beauty around you and in Nature and to be with whatever (and whomever) you find beautiful. This is the perfect antidote to noticing the negative and to constantly dealing with what needs healing.

Here is an exercise to honor beauty and your whole experience of the natural world. It is a fun thing to do either alone or with your Distant Healing group.

exercise 58 **HONORING BEAUTY AND THE NATURAL WORLD**

If possible, practice this exercise outdoors. Take yourself somewhere that you find especially beautiful. If you can't get out, study a beautiful photo or picture first. If you are unable to take up the bodily positions described, the exercise may still be done through your mental intention and visualization.

- Lie down with your back touching the ground. Have your legs slightly apart, arms relaxed by your sides, hands with palms up. Relax your body and breathe naturally.

- Being aware of the ground and the Earth that nurtures you, breathe in the Light through the whole top surface of your body. Take your time with this exercise.

- As you lie on your back, be aware that every plant, with its roots in the soil, pushes up into the light with its growing tip. Being aware of your connection to the plant world, carefully breathe the Light into the tips of your fingers and toes.

- Still lying on your back, be aware of the waters of the Earth and the creatures that live in them.

- Turn over and rest comfortably on the front of your body, with your arms bent at the elbows and palms resting on the ground in line with your head. Being aware of the creatures that travel over the Earth, breathe the Light into the whole back surface of your body.

- Being aware of the creatures that live under the Earth, breathe the Light into the whole back surface of your body again.

exercise continues >

- When you feel ready, stand up and fold your arms across your heart center, then slowly open them, completely extending your arms on a level with your shoulders. Being aware of all the beings that fly, breathe the Light into your heart center.

- Relax your arms by your sides. Check that your feet are shoulder-width apart, with your knees gently flexed. Slowly raise your arms, with the palms upward, to form a Y shape. Being aware of the trees, breathe the Light into your palms. Be aware of your "branches," your "trunk," and your "roots."

- Relax your arms by your sides again. Spend a few moments with this experience.

- In a group situation, this would be a good time to have a group hug!

Personal Energetic Health and Hygiene

As long as you follow the guidelines of this book, you will learn to function as a Distant Healer safely, effectively, and confidently.

Looking after your heart center is as important as looking after your physical heart. Similarly, your personal energetic health and hygiene are as necessary as keeping your body clean, flexible, and vigorous. This is maintained by carrying out the clearing, closing down, and protection exercises whenever you have concluded your work—before going to sleep, before going out and mixing with other people, and before a leisure or sporting activity (see in Chapter 5). You may be surprised at how open your subtle energy system is after reading or working with this book!

Keeping a Journal

Your Distant Healing journal will act like the best friend you need to confide in on your healing journey. As well as a useful record of what happens and charting your development as an energy worker, it is the place for other relevant comments, insights, dream material, and anything else that has a bearing on your work. But words may not always be the way you want to log your experiences. Sometimes a drawing, painting, or some other kind of creative work will be far more expressive.

Looking back on your journal can be a rewarding experience. You will have a fascinating personal record that shows how you engaged with *Distant Healing*. You may discover new abilities, new possibilities, and new friends.

I thank you for the work that you will do to help *all our relations*.

Acupuncture An energy therapy that uses the activation, by special metal needles, of energy points on the etheric meridians; common to Chinese Medicine.

Allopathic Contemporary medicine, particularly medicine using drugs in the treatment of illness.

Aura The total energetic emanation of the human being, including the physical, etheric, and other energy zones. The human energy field.

Breath The main way that we take in the life force; therefore considered to be sacred by many cultures from ancient times. A *kahuna* healer from Hawaii told me that the mystical meaning behind the greeting *aloha* (in the presence of the breath of life) is the wish to share *ha* (sacred breath).

Chakra A common term for a subtle energy center. From Sanskrit, *chakram*, or "wheel." The whirling vortex of energy looks somewhat like a turning wheel.

Distant Healing Healing when the subject is at a distance from the healer. When capitalized, refers to the particular form and techniques outlined in this book.

Earth When capitalized, refers to our planet from the Distant Healing point of view as a being in its own right.

Earth family The other beings that share the Earth with us.

Energy In Distant Healing, a force directed by, and emanating from, the Source. Spirit is the energy of the Source. Compared with this level of energy, the physical body has a vastly lower frequency.

Energy center A subtle structure, detected in the etheric body, designed to allow the flow of subtle energies into and out of the human energy field. The subject of Chapter 8.

Etheric The energetic level next to the physical at which energy vibrates at a higher frequency. Acts as the bridging zone between the physical and the subtle and is the support system for the physical body. From the ancient Greek term *ether*, which refers to the upper regions of the atmosphere, or heaven. Seers of the time witnessed that, on passing over, people carried on being in their "heavenly" or etheric body.

Higher Self The human soul; the indwelling spiritual force of the human being.

Life force The vital energy, essential to life, conducted by the subtle energy system. The same as *prana* (Sanskrit), *qi* (Chinese), and *ki* (Japanese).

Light When capitalized, another word for the Source or Oneness (which some call God). An aspect of spiritual energy. A force that encourages healing and enlightenment.

Love When capitalized, another word for the Source or Oneness. A force that encourages healing and integration.

Meridian A channel of subtle energy conduction in the etheric body.

Nature When capitalized, the Source manifesting as the natural world.

Oneness When capitalized, another word for the Source (which some call God). Describes the sacred unity of all that is.

Patient A conventional therapeutic term that simply distinguishes the person being helped from the healer.

Personality The self; the physical consciousness of the self that tends to see itself as separate from all that is—the natural world and the Source or Oneness.

Polarity balance The energy systems of living things, including humans, have two aspects or polarities: the receptive (often erroneously termed the "feminine") and the emissive (often erroneously termed the "masculine"). The possibility of receiving and giving out energy ensures its cyclic nature. Human health and well-being depend on maintaining a balance between the two energy streams. Whether this is the case affects the rest of the Earth and the Earth family.

Qi Gong The Chinese system of exercises where breath and movement are used to enhance the intake of *qi*, the life force.

Self See Personality.

Source When capitalized, another term for Oneness, which some call God, the Creator. The source of all energies.

Subtle energy In this book, energy vibrating at a higher frequency than physical matter. Such energy, traveling at a velocity beyond the speed of light, behaves in very different ways from those physical energies at present known to most science (see William Tiller in Further Reading, page 213, and Web Resources, page 217).

Subtle energy medicine Any therapy that works primarily with the subtle energy system to bring balance and/or harmony to the subject. Distant Healing is such a healing modality.

Subtle energy system The coordinated system of the etheric body, comprising the energy centers and their etheric network links and the other zones of the energy field.

Further Reading

Angelo, Jack. *Hands-On Healing.* Rochester, VT: Healing Arts Press, 1997.

Angelo, Jack. *Your Healing Power: A Comprehensive Guide to Channeling Your Healing Energy.* London: Piatkus Books, 1994/2007.

Angelo, Jack, and Angelo, Jan. *The Spiritual Healing Handbook: How to Develop Your Healing Powers and Increase Your Spiritual Awareness.* London: Piatkus Books, 2007.

Arrien, Angeles. *The Four-Fold Way: Walking the Paths of the Warrior, Teacher, Healer, and Visionary.* New York: HarperSanFrancisco, 1993.

Barnes, Simon. "No Island Is an Island," *Birds* (magazine of the Royal Society for the Protection of Birds), vol. 21, no. 4, 2006.

Dossey, Larry. *Healing Beyond the Body: Medicine and the Infinite Reach of the Mind.* Boston and London: Shambhala, 2001.

Dossey, Larry. *Healing Words: The Power of Prayer and the Practice of Medicine.* New York: HarperSanFrancisco, 1993.

Gerber, Dr. Richard. *Vibrational Medicine.* Santa Fe, NM: Bear & Company, 1988/1996.

Gerber, Dr. Richard, *Vibrational Medicine for the 21st Century.* London: Piatkus Books, 2000.

Krippner, S., and Welch P. *Spiritual Dimensions of Healing.* New York: Irvington Publications, 1992.

Lovelock, James. *Gaia: A New Look at Life on Earth.* Oxford and New York: Oxford University Press, 1979.

Maclean, Dorothy. *To Honor the Earth.* New York: HarperSanFrancisco, 1991.

Margulis, Lynn. *The Symbiotic Planet: A New Look at Evolution.* New York: Basic Books, 1998.

McElroy, Susan Chernak. *Animals as Teachers and Healers.* New York: New Sage Press, 1996.

Pearl, Dr. Eric. *The Reconnection.* New York and London: Hay House, 2001.

Pecci, Ernest F., and Tiller, William A. *Science and Human Transformation: Subtle Energies, Intentionality, and Consciousness.* Walnut Creek, CA: Pavior Publishing, 1997.

Suzuki, David, and Knudtson, Peter. *Wisdom of the Elders.* New York and London: Bantam Books, 1992.

Tiller, William A. "What Are Subtle Energies?" *Journal of Scientific Exploration*, vol. 7, no. 3, 1993.

Tiller, William A., Dibble, Walter, and Kohane, Michael. *Conscious Acts of Creation*. Walnut Creek, CA: Pavior Publishing, 2001.

Walsch, Neale Donald. *Communion with God*. London: Hodder & Stoughton, 2000.

Wilcox, Joan Parisi. *Keepers of the Ancient Knowledge: The Mystical World of the Q'ero Indians of Peru*. London and Boston: Element Books, 1999.

www.alternative-therapies.com Website of *Alternative Therapies in Health and Medicine* magazine (US)

www.caduceus.info Website of *Caduceus* magazine—"healing for people, community, and planet" (UK)

www.circleofcompassion.net Website of Circle of Compassion; "exploring peaceable choices for the planet and all who share it" (US)

www.contemplativemind.org Website of the Center for Contemplative Mind in Society (US)

www.dosseydossey.com Official website of Dr. Larry Dossey, who has written extensively on the power of intention and intentional prayer

www.ecolo.org Ecological website, with section endorsed by Professor James Lovelock

www.hayfoundation.org Website of Hay Foundation work

www.issseem.com Website of the International Society for the Study of Subtle Energies and Energy Medicine—a meeting place for scientists, mystics, and energy practitioners

www.jackangelo.com Official website of Jack Angelo, writer and teacher in the fields of subtle energy medicine, natural spirituality, and world spiritual traditions

www.nccam.nih.gov Official website of the National Center for Complementary and Alternative Medicine (US)

www.nfsh.org.uk Website of the National Federation of Spiritual Healers; leading nondenominational teaching and lobbying organization, with international links (UK)

www.noetic.org Website of the Institute of Noetic Sciences (IONS); founded in 1973, IONS has a number of projects involving distant healing and intentional prayer and an extensive bibliography of scientific studies on distant healing (US)

www.realityshifters.com Website "for those who know (or are beginning to suspect) that our thoughts and feelings shift reality"; information on studies about distant healing (US)

www.resurgence.org Website of *Resurgence* magazine, linking ecology, spirituality, art, and culture (UK)

www.rspb.org.uk Website of the Royal Society for the Protection of Birds, an organization also dedicated to environmental protection in general

www.soundstrue.com Website of audio courses, books, DVDs, and music for personal and spiritual transformation

www.spiritualityhealth.com Website of *Spirituality and Health* magazine (US)

www.thereconnection.com Website of Dr. Eric Pearl's work

www.tillerfoundation.com Website of Professor William Tiller's work

www.wholistichealingresearch.com Website of Holistic Healing
  Research, hosted by leading researcher Dr. Daniel Benor